WALDO FRANK
IN AMERICA HISPANA

WALDO FRANK
IN AMERICA HISPANA

INSTITUTO DE LAS ESPAÑAS

EN LOS ESTADOS UNIDOS

NEW YORK

1930

Copyright, 1930
by the Instituto de las Españas

Printed in the U. S. A. by
Lancaster Press, Inc., Lancaster, Pa.

CONTENTS

PAGE

Contents

FOREWORD

The INSTITUTO DE LAS ESPAÑAS has wished
to record in the publication of this volume, one
of the cardinal events in the intellectual relations between the United States and the Hispanic world: Waldo Frank's trip to various
Spanish American countries. We have thought
that the Americans should know what one of
their countrymen has done in South America,
and how our neighbors, the Spanish-speaking
Americans, have responded to his labor.

The reading of these pages will, we hope, reveal the enduring value of everything connected
with Waldo Frank's trip. Waldo Frank is a
man of letters, a thinker, who went to Hispano-
America, not in any official capacity, but with
only his own ideas and his own personality.
The value of his ideas and his personality does
not come from the fact that they are representative of all North Americans or many of
them, but, on the contrary, because they are his
own, because of their originality. Many may
not share them; the INSTITUTO, in publishing
this book, does not assume that the viewpoints
of Waldo Frank and the divers Hispano-
American authors are the only possible ones.
Its purpose is to comply with its fundamental

aim of supporting and fostering all intellectual
activities between these two cultures, without
attempting to adopt or impose any criterion.

The ideas of Waldo Frank will always have
the value inherent in sincere and originally conceived ideas, and will serve as a stimulus to
action in others, whether similar or combative.
For this reason his trip through the Hispano-
American countries, of which this book is an
account, was not reflected in official acts and
ceremonies, but in the expression of thoughts
and ideas of the thinkers and writers of
Hispano-America, each of whom reveals to us
in his comments and criticism, not only what
he, individually, thinks of Frank and of the
problems of America, but the total reaction
of the Hispano-American mind to Frank's interpretation of his America.

This is the theme of general and lasting
interest to which the INSTITUTO wishes to call
attention by the publication of some articles
selected from the great number which Frank's
trip elicited. The writers of these articles are
intellectual figures of the greatest prestige in
their own countries and in the Hispanic com-
monwealth. These constitute the major part
of this book. We are not including Waldo
Frank's lectures because his ideas on Hispano-
America will soon appear in a new book. We
include only one of his addresses which reveals

his attitude toward, rather than his ideas on Hispano-America. But as the events of his trip which motivated the aforesaid commentaries and studies should also be known, we have asked one of our members, Mr. M. J. Benardete of Hunter College—to whom the INSTITUTO here wishes to express its gratitude for his editorial labor on this volume—, to write a brief account of it and point out its significance.

INSTITUTO DE LAS ESPAÑAS

WALDO FRANK, TO
HISPANO–AMERICA

"Through Buenos Aires have passed the most enlightened lecturers of the world. The great intellectuals of Europe were wont to speak to the Argentinians if not as mature persons to younger ones, at least as outsiders. But recently the North American (sic!) writer Waldo Frank has put a stop to that practice. He has spoken to the Argentinians as from within; that is to say, he has placed himself in the attitude of the American who speaks on equal terms with other Americans, and who speaks to them, moreover, about the destiny, responsibility, and spiritual mission of America, in relation to the problems of the new culture which appears in the world.

"This happy thought of the great North American writer has received its deserved reward. Although the public of Buenos Aires is accustomed to manifest lavishly its good will and its applause to all the notable representatives of the mind who reach its shore, toward Waldo Frank its applause has gone the limit, to such a point that it goes beyond all that has been known up to now. We can well be permitted to call it an exception; or we may even use the word *record*, since we are dealing with something genuinely American."

This is a sober summary of what took place during Waldo Frank's triumphal lecture tour through South America. It is taken from an article in the January 15 issue of the Madrid daily *A. B. C.*, by the well-known writer José María Salaverría. Professor Federico de Onís of Columbia University, our most successful exponent of Spanish literature and the culture subsuming it, confirms this judgment in unmistakable terms. The present chronicler, placed in a strategic position, had the opportunity to read thousands upon thousands of agate lines appearing in hundreds of newspaper articles and in a score of magazines. The articulation of the effect produced is both amazing and revelatory of a unique event in the hardly begun cultural relations between this country and Hispano-America. Before interpreting this happening, the facts in bare outline should have precedence. Waldo Frank gave over forty lectures in the high lands and low lands of Spanish-speaking America. At its University and other centres, Mexico City heard him in the summer of last year. Buenos Aires, besides opening its University to him in most generous fashion and paying him, to boot, munificently, gave him access to its exclusive clubs and cultural societies. The Argentinian cities Córdoba, Rosario, La Plata, Tucumán, Santiago del Estero invited him to deliver his spiritual message in person, just as he had done in numerous lectures at their capital. Subsequently, Lima in Peru, La Paz in Bolivia, and Habana in Cuba heard Waldo Frank explain in Spanish (which he has mastered in uncanny fashion) the chief ideas he champions.

Translations of the most important articles relating to this event, appearing in the magazines *1930*, *Nosotros*, *Síntesis*, *Crítica*, *Diógenes*, etc. and in the great dailies of Mexico City, Buenos Aires, Lima, La Paz, Sao Paulo, Habana, are included in this book to which the American reader can turn, to familiarize himself with the response evoked by Waldo Frank's spiritual message. The sepulchral silence maintained by our own newspapers and magazines over this event, the resistance shown on the part of our intellectual minorities when an attempt was made to arouse them from their lethargy, is a most curious commentary on the trend of events in the United States. In spite of the fine banquet tendered to Waldo Frank at the Hotel Roosevelt on February 17, to celebrate his epoch-making trip, we have not yet gauged the import of our spiritual rapproachement with Hispano-America.

II

Aeroplane flights of good will from the United States to the countries south of us; Ambassador Morrow's skillful diplomacy in bringing about a better understanding between the governments of the United States and of Mexico, and his good offices employed to effect a modus vivendi between Church and State in Mexico; the settlement of the Tacna-Arica decades-old snag, again through the diplomatic channels of this country; the visit of Mr. Hoover as President-elect to divers of those countries that speak Spanish; the creation of an Argentinian-United States Cultural Centre in Buenos Aires; the Guggenheim Scholarship Fund to enable South and Central American students to continue their studies in this country and to enable students of the United States to do research work in those countries—these acts and gestures of amity within the past few years, emanating from this country on behalf of Hispano-America, are contributing to create an atmosphere of benevolence among the governments and business interests of those countries towards the United States. Investments of American money amounting to a billion dollars already and the commerce between Hispano-America and the United States on the scale of billions do most effectively help to bring about a non-hostile frame of mind.

Our moving picture films disseminated from the Rio Grande to Tierra del Fuego serve as prepotent agents by placing before the common people of those countries the meaning we attach to sports, wealth, work, sanitation, comfort, the regard in which we hold women and children, our ideals of heroism, love, what we consider villainous acts, our sentimentalisms,—all these are put across by means of images in contexts intended not to teach but to amuse. They do, however, in the long run bind the Hispano-Americans to us through the bonds of our common humanity; through our moving pictures we are Americanizing the rank and file of those people who share America with us.

There is a small class of people, the intelligentsia, in each of these Hispano-American countries, who do not participate in the beneficial effects of the new spirit manifested by the people and government of this country towards their countries. Through their reading of history and their familiarity with the *yankifobia* found in their best poet Rubén Darío (ominously, a Nicaraguan) and their chief thinker Enrique Rodó, these intellectual minorities have very definite notions as to why they should hate the deeds of American imperialism and be ill-disposed towards the cultural attainments and possibilities of the United States.

Rubén Darío, addressing himself to Roosevelt, said of this country:

"You are the United States
You are the future invader
Of that ingenuous America in whom glows indigenous blood,
And which still prays to Jesus Christ and speaks Spanish."

In the same poem, he hurled this accusation which will be for long years a summation of the United States for Spanish-speaking America: "You are rich. To the cult of Hercules, you join the cult of Mammon."

These words are in harmony with *The Breviary of South-American Youth*, the name given to *Ariel*, Rodo's brilliant essay on the meaning of culture. (There is an English translation by F. J. Stimson.) The Uruguayan Emerson submits the utilitarianism of this country to an acid test, which burns many holes into it.

Dislike of the United States is nurtured also through their cultural importations from Europe. Ever since the Armistice, the mills of hatred have ground very fine overseas. The ideas and aesthetic of Hispano-America belong to the aristocratic tradition of the mother countries. Though they admire and appreciate Emerson, Thoreau, Poe, and Whitman, the United States of the Golden Days, these intellectuals have no use for the culture values of this country cast in such original moulds. The pragmatism of James rather than that of Peirce, the instrumentalism of our efficiency experts rather than the philosophy of John Dewey, the practical inventions of Edison rather than the highly scientific achievements of men like Michelson—these are what they know of the United States via Europe. The deep thoughts of Royce on loyalty, the liberalizing concepts of Santayana on the Life of Reason, the tumbling uncertainties of a soul in search and travail like that of Henry Adams, the humanism of revolutionary depths of Professor Babbitt, the prophetic vision of men like Stieglitz in his photography and his way of life, the unique paintings of Georgia O'Keeffe and John Marin,—such positive achievements as these in art, philosophy, and life which are making the culture of this country, were up to the time of Waldo Frank's trip, closed books to these minorities of South America.

Misunderstanding of the United States breeds animosities in this class, which find expression in song, essay, editorial, and social gathering. All official attempts to cement bonds between the United States and Hispano-America will not endure. Not until the intellectuals are disposed to look with sympathy on us will we gain their hearts and minds. The intellectuals

of Hispano-America can be approached through
their kind, their peers. It is because we were
asked to send our first intellectual, Waldo
Frank, to Hispano-America that his visit and
lecture tour are of such tremendous significance.

III

When Enrique Rodó and Rubén Darío
visioned the United States—one the utilitarianism, the other the imperialism of our foreign
policy in Hispano-America—little did they
dream that the day was soon to dawn when dis-
comfiture and malaise over the Power of the
country and all its creatures were to be felt by
the most sensitive groups of our land. An
America of dissatisfaction, an America that
feels a lack, an America that is unhappy is
what Hispano-America never had the opportunity to know. Fear and envy of the United
States obfuscated them to the America in
search of a consistent self, accepted on the
highest levels of spiritual consciousness. Waldo
Frank brought to them this America in dis-
sension, this America of negation and denial,
coupled with the vision of our need to co-
operate, spiritually and culturally, with Hispano-America. For many years before going
to the peoples south of us, he had trained himself to speak for them by maturing his idea of an
America capable of creating an original civili-

zation which would be the summation of the mystical tradition of the Mediterranean Basin. As a student of philosophy, he knew that concepts without percepts are empty. That he might meet our copartners in America, he needed to know the source of their being. Just as Henry Adams delved into medieval times to plumb the significance of the mathematico-technological culture of the nineteenth and twentieth centuries, first grasping to the full the bloom-freshness of St. Michel and Chartres before writing his moving chapter on The Dynamo and the Virgin (Cf. *The Education of Henry Adams*), in the same manner did Waldo Frank study Spain, the Spain which dared to be medieval when France, England, Italy, Germany were breaking with their past. He came to love her. While he prepared for the better comprehension of both the United States and Hispano-America, Spain helped him to see how it was possible that a nation, at the time of the very beginnings of modern history, supremely cool in her judgment, could throw her lot on the side of the realization of a religious self, when other clamoring selves (the Renaissance possibility on the level of reason and sensuousness and the Protestant choice on the side of freedom of conscience) promised economic well-being and conservation to the goods possessed. That a nation can construct for herself a systematized character just as an individual, Frank learned from Spain. This lesson once learned made Waldo Frank persist in his espousal of a *willed* America. And through his symphonic orchestration of the essences of the soul of Spain, Waldo Frank created for himself the credentials of the American Ambassador to Hispano-America. His *Virgin Spain* (1926), translated by León Felipe, a great poet, had won for him the attention and affection of the Spanish-speaking intellectuals of America before he made his visit. Not even Havelock Ellis had come so near to capturing in luminous images the eternal modalities of the Spanish sensibility and ideology.

As a novelist and essayist, he gave himself only American themes. His dedication to the evocation of a country freed from its mechanical jungle and exorcised from its obsessions in the pursuit of power, received final form in his *The Re-Discovery of America* (1929), subtitled *An Introduction to a Philosophy of American Life*. (It appeared in instalments in The New Republic during the year 1928.)

Some question the premises, others the inferences of his book, but few or none can question his competence to talk on the things of the United States. In the forty-odd lectures addressed to Hispano-America, Waldo

Frank appeared as a messenger of the spiritual happenings in this country, and as an apostle of the new dispensation which can bring wholeness or holiness to our diseased wills and dispersive, destructive selves, and as a paraclete of the union of this country with Hispano-America, to effect a real living organism out of a geographical entity that is swiftly becoming a single economic one.

IV

As has been suggested above, Waldo Frank endeavored to bring about through his lectures of last year in Hispano-America the insinuation of a new image of his country into the minds of Hispanic minorities who for long had been hypnotized by a distorted, grimacing caricature of the United States.   Divested of the offensive complex of the traveling American, whose pocket is lined with the magic of his dollars, he spoke to his audiences in a minor key.   In all humility and contrition for the deeds of his government, he opened to view the sore spots infesting our apparently healthy body politic. Deploring the irresistible onrush of our imperialism over their countries, he begged their indulgence that he might show its source. The manoeuvres of our cruisers in their waters and the infiltration of dollars in their lands were simply the triumph of unregenerate forces at home. If they have been smarting under the workings of unconscionable exploitation, the people of the United States, on the other hand, have been the victims of the same system which not only begets imperialism, but is the incubator of an environment that is inimical to the good life, in spite of its economic promise. Waldo Frank analyzed to their amazement the American scene; where they expected a paeon to the machine, he showed the excrescences of the mechanical jungle; where they imagined wealth to be hailed as synonymous with blessings, he pointed out the shrivelled lives resulting from the constant worship of Power. Other repulsive traits of ours he traced to the fact that our politics are inane, our churches sterile, our arts insipid, our education mechanical, our journalism venal, our women at odds with their very womanhood, our cities planless, our countrysides imitative of the city, our minorities impotent.

Waldo Frank was, however, very careful to point out that the excrescences of our machine civilization are not essentially peculiar to us. Our climate, our land, the very substrata of our population gathered from all over the world, are in contradiction to the evils corroding us. What characterizes us is directly traceable to the dissolution of the medieval Christian synthesis. Many factors tended

to make the cultural fragments of the tacitly
assumed whole of European Christendom
evolve into monstruous proportions in our land.
Quantification, mechanization, standardization
obey the revolutionary application of the will
to the acquisition of power, on behest of the personal lusts.

In a derogatory sense, our enemies abroad
and our tortured critics at home have dubbed
these traits of our ethos "Americanism."
Waldo Frank, with great conviction and always
in a tone vibrating with religious feeling, made
the point that what is undesirable in our civilization (those evils as enumerated above), that
is to say, this so called "Americanism," is also,
let us say it without spinning paradoxes, the
evil of Europe and Hispano-America writ
large. Lest there be misinterpretations, cau-
tiously he let his Argentinian audiences, in
particular, realize in his penetrative lecture
"The Problem of the Relations between the
Two Americas" that if he with aching heart,
operated on the living flesh of our America, it
was because he knew our America best and
could speak convincingly of her, and also
because the tearing down process evident in
his analyses obeyed the larger vision of building
up, out of the elements of promise in our land,
the new world for which so many vision-
haunted men and women have been dreaming,

fighting, working. And sanctioned by his sincerity he fearlessly told Argentina and the rest of Hispano-America that they were under Caliban as much as we.

Hispano-America and Europe dance to the hypnotic music of "Americanism" not because any satanic prestidigitation is at work, but because they too are in decomposition like ourselves. It requires very little effort to "Americanize" any atomic individual or nation. The resistances of a spiritual quality are lacking. Disintegrated individuals are at home today everywhere. Really inconceivable is the "Americanization" of a Mahatma Gandhi in that sense, for no other reason than that he lives as the conscious part of a projected whole.

Waldo Frank, having given his hearers his devastating criticism of our mechanical jungle, as a phase of the atomization of man everywhere in the world, succinctly pointed out that we must acquire spiritual health through the sense of the whole. This potent idea of Frank's textures the constructive part of his envisagement of the New World in America. Into its details we cannot enter here. Suffice it to say that by this basic ideal he means to suggest that methodology whereby we can conjure away the deleterious effects in our culture emanating from our possessive, personalistic or separatistic selves. We must

begin by self-reform or the structurization of
the self in accordance with the images inducing
in us that type of behavior dictated by our
living understanding that we are the integers or
parts of a whole in which we find the complete
realization of our spiritual weal.

We are all menaced by the life that surrounds
us and the life we actually lead. We North
Americans as well as Hispano-Americans are
living in chaos. Frank told our Spanish-
speaking brethren that the minorities of both
Americas must continue the painful but liberating training of our disjunctive selves in order to
bring about the reign of love. Love is the
antithesis of Power; it brings subordination; it
brings the lover and the beloved together for
the purpose of creation. It gives, it dedicates
the lover to the consecration of the loved one,
it does not demand or impose like Power.
Our America and their America can be won
over to the mystic tradition latent in our
respective cultural inheritances through the
efforts of the anointed ones in conjunction with
their groups.

"The American chaos has all the elements
for the creation of a new world, a world more
complete than any other in past history.
Because all the worlds of the past, Europe,
Asia, Africa, even Atlantis have brought
their dissolution and their seed to our American
chaos."

"Men and women similar to those I have in mind, in Argentina, in the Andes, in Brazil, in Cuba, in Mexico, and in the United States can capture that American chaos. The chaos and distemper of our modern world await men and women such as those among you." *

If we bear in mind the intellectual acumen evident in his analyses, and the apostolic fervor palpitating in words similar to those quoted above, we are not at a loss to understand how Waldo Frank sent a religious thrill through the hearts and minds of the best men and women of Hispano-America.

M. J. BENARDETE

* Cf. "Mi primer mensaje a la America Hispana," Revista de Occidente, Madrid, p. 269. This book contains the most important lectures which Waldo Frank delivered in the countries South of us.

I. A BANQUET IN BUENOS AIRES

The Homage of Argentina
to Waldo Frank

The banquet given last night in honor of
Waldo Frank took on the intense form of an
extraordinary public act—of an occasion rarely
equalled among us. A group of distinguished
people representative of our intellectual world
surrounded the broad tables, over which presided, in the midst of a crowded assembly, the
patriarchal portrait of Walt Whitman. Young
men of letters and the best known names in the
artistic circles of this city paid, during the
whole affair, a homage full and simple to the
illustrious author of *City Block*.

The seat of honor was occupied by the North
American writer, at whose right were seated the
president of the Instituto Cultural Argentino
Norte Americano, the organizer of the function,
Dr. Alfredo Colmo; the Ambassador of Mexico,
Don Alfonso Reyes; Dr. Coriolano Alberini,
ex-dean of the University of Buenos Aires;
and at the left of Waldo Frank were the
president of the Society of Writers, Don
Leopoldo Lugones, the dean of the Faculty of
Philosophy and Letters, Dr. Emilio Ravignani;
Doctors José Arce and Enrique Gil and Don
Alberto Gerchunoff.

In the name of the Instituto Cultural Argentino Norte-Americano, Dr. Alfredo Colmo

delivered a speech which opened with these words:

"In our desire for an interchange of cultures, the Institute, which has already made known to the United States its purpose and its password, wished to bring to this country the word of a representative North American. Here lay a difficult problem. We could find in the fields of science, art, the novel, criticism, history, poetry, philosophy, great figures of almost world-reputation, figures such as Michelson, Sinclair Lewis, Mencken, Professor Babbitt, Dreiser, Sandburg, John Dewey, Robert Frost, and many others equally worthy. We preferred Waldo Frank because he stands out among those named, and because, among other reasons, we find him to be deeply in touch with our own American spirit, concerning which he has expressed judgments of the greatest excellence and originality."

. . . Dr. Colmo concluded, saying: "Let us fervently hope then, that this analyst of events, this creator of ideas, for whom the union of the Americas is a postulate to be realized above all others, as a supreme vision of the spiritual synthesis of nations, will find here the foundation stones for that superb edifice to which he aspires. In extending to him our cordial and fraternal greetings, let us open to him our hearts: that he may see us in our pristine naturalness, that he may know us in the most deeply hidden aspects of our will; and that he may take from us the quintessential understanding which will serve him as the basis for his conclusions and for his hopes on our behalf.

Meanwhile, as we eagerly await his word and teaching, let us limit ourselves to saying to him: Waldo Frank, enter our house and make it your home, because our home is not only ours, but also the house and home of him who, like you, is our friend, our brother and our master."

La Nación, Buenos Aires

The Address of Leopoldo Lugones

My dear Sir: I bring you my most cordial greetings and that of the Argentine Society of Writers. Allow me to take advantage of this ceremony to make a few profitable points: we shall begin by avoiding vain words which are sins against religion and beauty. Our tutelar deity should be bare as light, and, like light, brilliant and chaste. Even as we desire to maintain ourselves in simple rejoicing in order better to receive you, we prefer, to any glorious offerings on the altar of Athena, the soft and intimate violets that the devotees of Aglaura, among them, Plato, brought to the nearby shrine. Seated upon a sweep of marble we shall celebrate this feast of friendship with a bunch of grapes and a handful of almonds. Conversation will be harmonious, and before us will stretch the serenity of a purple sea.

He who knows, as you, how to depict peoples and men, grasping their very soul, and judging them with impartiality since you begin by judging yourself, is a bright messenger of fellowship. We lack this good fellowship, and that is why we continue to suffer a great misunderstanding. We are two ignorant Americas, although we are aware of the desirability of understanding each other. We lack, and we need, understanding and talent, enthusiasm and rectitude, wit and prudence. You possess these qualities and that is why we have summoned you. There is also in you a comprehension similar to that of the Latin peoples, which is an hereditary predisposition of Israel from Philo to Heine. And our peoples are both Latin and Catholic. Our mental formation is therefore esthetic, and requires the appreciation of an artist. There is no one like you, sir, to fulfill this obligation. Truth and even politics are, for you, modalities of beauty. If this were not so, how would you have been able to discover the poet in Lincoln and the politician in Whitman? We were also interested in the fact that you were a man of progressive ideas; a man of the "Left," as they say today; an anarchist, if you please. So much the better. It could not but be an advantage for a man of talent to be free. What could a man possessing genius for communication be, other than an agitator? It was an imperialistic poet, militaristic and conservative at the same time, who decreed forever: "Mens agitat molem"—the mind moves the mass. Ideas are not harmful except in the wicked. Even more, they are harmful *for* the wicked. It seems good to us, then, that you disagree with many of your admirers, and I prepare myself to be the flint to your steel, if matters come to that. So you will appreciate us without circumlocutions. And to strike a spark from you is, in my estimation, like striking forth beauty.

On the other hand, as good Argentinians, we know you to be a good American. That is enough for us. I am very much inclined to say that a good patriot is a constructor: the contrary, then, of a methodical resident in old houses; and the contrary, as well, of a methodical demolisher. We have a whole continent to build, and in more than one extensive region we have hardly as yet begun to gather the materials. We would exceed the folly of Babel if we began to quarrel even before working it out on blue print.

But it is certain that we misunderstand each other. Before anything else, it is necessary to rectify this situation. Very well, then, the best way to understand one another is to find out where lies our misunderstanding. I do not pretend to speak in the name of any country nor to refer to any but my own. I consider any continental representation impertinent and vague, especially if one were to bestow it upon himself. The collaboration most useful to our common purpose consists in each of us minding his own business.

It seems to me, then, that our initial error

here has consisted in believing that the thing
most worthy of imitating in the United States
was its Constitution. This can be explained.
The nineteenth century was, above all, political, because it believed that in politics lay the
secret of human happiness. We attributed
universal efficacy to that law which was, on
the contrary, a very peculiar creation of the
United States; and we introduced it without
hesitation, overlooking what was really imita-
ble: their method of work, as applicable to the
construction of a country. In spite of appear-
ances, then, that was a blunder—a blunder
that could not be undone, because it was so
deeply rooted. One example alone will suffice.

Scarcely could there be institutions more
genuinely American than the Supreme Court
and the Senate, each one an invention of that
people's national genius, nourished by two
springs that here do not exist at all: the Biblical
inspiration that brings to mind regarding that
tribunal the government of the judges of Israel,
and the argumentative genius that in private
conversation, in theatrical tragedies, and in
the family and religion, equilibrates the British
structure. It may be said that everything is
parliamentary in Anglo-Saxon countries. This
argumentative criterion of theirs based on the
utility of reaching an understanding, for the
purpose of acting in agreement; that is to say,

for the sake of the greatest common good, conforms equally with the English Parliament whose members do not fight with one another, and with the Congress of the United States, which, among all those of the world, registers the least number of deadly challenges.

Among us, there is nothing like that. Our Christianity is not Biblical, but Catholic: a conciliation between moral liberty and theological authority, which only demands respect for its symbols. Our parliamentary debates are esthetic spectacles. People attend them to hear good speaking; and so the outcome of the deliberation is not a conviction, but a triumph. No sooner has elocution disappeared from our Congress, than it loses its reason for existing. It is beginning, now, to disappear.

That is why we are authoritarians and personalists. These characteristics, as we see them reacting in nations similarly constituted, will work in favor of a general rectification. This is where the intervention of a defect peculiar to the Anglo-Saxon America may possibly disunite us, namely: the Puritan proselytism by virtue of which Wilson wished to impose upon the whole world the democratic system of government. Thus there is in existence since his administration, the purpose of not recognizing in America any government of irregular origin lacking the sanction of votes.

This attitude is, for us, a very great impertinence. We understand his good intentions, as in the Monroe Doctrine, which is another declaration of a missionary character. But it annoys us because it wishes to impose a good upon us, when our conception of liberty interprets it as their right of doing us harm. Because of our artistic disposition, we do not wish liberty to serve us the compacts of life, but to give us glory. And this arises also from deep causes.

The Conquest, from which both Americas proceed, was in your case an enterprise and in ours an adventure. For this reason the former America prospered before the latter. Only now are we beginning to engage in the exploitation of our soil. For this reason it is necessary that your America help us with her superior experience, without obstructing us with her ideology. Let us begin to build our house from our own plan. It seems to me that the moment has arrived for substituting the formula of America for Americans, by that of America for America. By this, let it be well understood; each one in his own way, without alliances and dogmas. Solely on behalf of life. Like a work of art.

I believe, sir, that in this we are agreed, and my initial evocation was an answer to that agreement. The construction that we spoke of will be an act of beauty; that is to say, of proportion and of serenity. I am with those who always have believed in the idealism of your great fatherland. It is now thirty-two years since my first poem hailed Whitman as among the heralds of human fellowship. It is now twelve years since the World War, when I called attention to the duty of Argentina to stick by the giant of the North in its noble hour of danger. Thus your "integral America" is also for me the idea of an artist.

All is of value, certainly, to the harmonious temple standing on vigorous columns: from the paving of the threshhold to the edge of the triglyph; and from the solitary worshipper who whispers his prayer in the shadow, to the burning incense that rises on the wings of its own perfume. . . .

La Nación, Buenos Aires

The Address of Waldo Frank

Friends: I thank Señor Colmo and Señor Lugones for the words which their generosity inspired them to speak tonight. I know but one way to thank you, you and those whom you represent: but one way to show you the gratitude I feel. It consists in trying with all my power to give to Argentina what I have been invited to give, and what I have come six thousand miles to give: the truth, the whole truth as I see it, concerning my country and the problems of relations between us.

The two representative men who have welcomed me this evening know very well that many of my opinions and convictions differ from their own. Do not think that they are unaware of this disagreement in its full extent. I acknowledge heartily and publicly how their action honors them, how indeed your own generosity honors you, since it is the generosity of the strong. I shall do what I can to be worthy of it, by saying what I have to say without compromise and without stint.

But you will not expect a formal discourse from me tonight. I want to feel that I am among friends—old friends, indeed, since it is a long time I have known you, in spirit and in letter. One does not deliver a speech to one's friends. One can be sure of their good will, but to deliver a speech to friends is an unforgivable offense. I am in need of your good will; and I am confident that I have it. For even though I feel at home with you, here, the fact is that I am far from being at home in your language. Yet I do not wish to speak English tonight—even if it might mean that you would all understand me better. It means so much to me to try to speak with you in Spanish, that I am certain you will permit this, and forgive my errors—above all my doubtless dreadful Castilian-North-American accent. Most readily, you will forgive me, since my impulse in speaking Spanish is to make me feel more at home with you. And you will forgive my Spanish since I have really never had much time to learn it. A few months—years ago in Spain, seven weeks recently in Mexico: that is all I have had to help me besides the reading of good books (many of them by you) and above all my love for the genius of Spain and of America-Hispana which is incarnate in your language. With all these good reasons, you will excuse me if I torture you, by torturing your tongue. Brothers are made—at times— to torture each other.

I am here, friends, primarily because I am **an** artist. I have not come to preach, or to pray, or to pry. I have come because what interests me more than all else in the world is *creation:* aesthetic, spiritual creation. And I have felt for long that there was something here which I needed, in my own terms and in my own humble way, to create. America is a potential organism: a potential Whole. Actually, up till now, it has been little more than a word. And America will be created by artists. By artists of all kinds: artists in thoughts, in words, in architecture, in plastic form, in music— artists in law, in relationship, and in action. Only artists can create America: and only to the extent that artists have accomplished their creative task can the statesmen and the critics carry on what has been created. Only to the extent that artists have created America, can the peoples of America experience America and enjoy it. And this, to me, is the ultimate goal: an America that will be realised, experienced, and enjoyed by the many American peoples.

You see how ambitious I am. I admit it. I do not care what measure of personal success I shall have, in my share of creating America. But I know that no other task seems worth while to me. There is no heroism in what I do; no sacrifice. I am simply working at the one job which pleases and thrills me most. It is the *working-at-it* which brings me satisfaction.

There are plenty of other things I might do,

in the modern world. I might go out to get rich, for instance: or to get as popular as possible: or to invite and indulge my senses. Or I might withdraw into an Ivory Tower, communing with a secret and superior Muse or with a god alien and aloof from the world. But long ago, such activities seemed to me far less worth while than the one which challenged me as an American: the challenge of all of us who are Americans. We are the sons of all the old worlds. There is not one culture, mediterranean, nordic, oriental, whose essence is not within us. But we are also the potential fathers of a new culture. And who would deny that there is greater joy in being a father than a son? The challenge is, then, to create this new world. And since it will be our creation—to be able to call it America, in truth.

You see, the task is one of art—in the largest, truest sense of art. Art implies beauty. But beauty means merely an entire consciousness of life: beauty means conscious participation *in* life. This America we must create shall therefore be more conscious, more alive—hence more beautiful—than any world of the past.

Take Greece, for instance—or India and Egypt. These were great worlds, once upon a time. But how small a part of the entire human organism of these worlds, participated in its consciousness and beauty! In Greece a few patricians rested their fine labors on a dark mass of slaves. In India and Egypt, castes of holy men alone had the light, and guarded it zealously from the dark blind masses. Not only were the vast majority of men barred from the conscious, active splendor of culture: most women were barred also. These were not cultures of humanity; they were cultures of class—of tiny, insolent minorities exploiting the Whole. And in most of the values and ideologies we have inherited, this exploitation, this dualism, this exclusiveness are implied. Not yet has the earth seen a race of men living integrally in the light together. But until that time comes, the human race will be diseased: it will be like a body whose mind is separate from it—a body in which some parts are nourished by food and light, while others are cut off and languish.

To bring about such a human culture America was founded. For the dream of this has always existed. The task seems to me so much more exciting than any other: the humblest share in this task seems to me so far more exalted than any other! Our problem then is to create MORE LIFE. That, deep down, is the essence of all art: more light and more life.

Man is still a larva, in comparison with his potentialities. Those who do not share this belief—who think that the capacity of man to grow is limited, and that the limit has been reached, will not care for what I shall say while I am in America Hispana. Take the dark egg that becomes the caterpillar: and the butterfly at last. Three stages. Man is still in the first—the egg stage. His capacities to know and to enjoy are as yet unhatched. He has not even begun to crawl;—the caterpillar stage is still beyond him. The period of splendor in the Sun—his eternal day in which he will spread his wings and fly—is far beyond. But every man who holds the vision of that day and works toward it, however vicariously and humbly, knowing that in the flesh he must yet die a larva—every such man in some miraculous way finds wings, finds the sun of life, finds that that eternal day is his.

You see, I am speaking to you openly: I want you to accept me as your brother. But under no false pretenses. I want you to understand that if I am a critic—a rather savage critic, my underlying impulse always is to achieve beauty—the beauty which lives in truth: to achieve life, more and more life—the life whose consciousness and whose experience we know as beauty.

I want to make one more point clear. I am an uncompromising critic of my country; so much so that strangers who have seen but a fragment of my work or fragmentary versions of it, have assumed that I am no lover of my country. Every critical work that I have written has been inspired by my love of my country, and has been inspired, besides, by my faith in the high destiny of my country. Were it not for this love and this faith, I should have abstained from writing criticism: I am far happier when I am writing a story or a novel. Were it not for this love and this faith, I should have taken the advice of many of my friends in Europe, who lack my love and my faith in the United States—and lived in Europe, like so many other American artists.

To a vast extent, the faults and vices of the United States are simply the common traits of the entire modern world: a world in chaos of transition. For, as I shall hope to show you, the entire era which proudly calls itself the modern era is essentially an era of chaos and transition. The modern traits are accentuated in the United States, because our energy, our tremendous will, our genius accentuate and render conspicuous everything we are and do. In the high will to create a new world, in the high energy to work for a new world, in the high capacity to achieve a new world, no part of America—no section of the earth—is superior to the United States. We have a tradition, mystic and exalted, which has not died since

4

the Jesuits and Puritans came to our northern shores. That tradition has changed and must still change its form: it is the tradition of an Ideal, which has never reached its goal. But the tradition and the ideal have not died. Our great writers of the past belonged to it; some at least of our statesmen (Lincoln, Jefferson, for instance) struggled to express it. And it is alive today.

All this I shall hope to make clear in my lectures. To describe indeed the heroic, tragic, ever renascent course of the American Ideal (and our need of all America to realise it) is the reason why I have come here. Tonight I wish merely to explain that if I must ruthlessly expose the failures and vices of modern life—accentuated in North American life, the reason is that only so can I reveal the promise and high destiny of my America and of all the American nations.

My love for my country is not official, not romantic. It does not depend on seeing only parts—and on ignoring others. It lives rather in the act of illumining the Whole. It is naturalistic, I hope. And if I am a mystic (as I have often been called), I am a naturalistic mystic.

I believe in life: not life when it soothes and cajoles me—but in life for what it is and—above all—for what it must become! I believe with Spinoza, that error and evil are but inadequate knowledge. As an artist, I am concerned in the creating of wholes. And I have come here to be able to share with you, henceforth, more intimately the creative task of our generation: which is to bring into being a Whole America.

Such an America, in which consciousness and conduct, however varied, will be universal; in which life, seen whole, will be synonymous with beauty, does not exist. Its birth would be the revelation for which all men are hungering today—the reality to make men know at last, that life is good.

La Nación, Buenos Aires

II. THE AUTHORS OF HISPANO-AMERICA ON WALDO FRANK

The Hispano-American press published hundreds of articles, reporting the lectures and discussing the significance of the visit of Waldo Frank. For several months, he was "first page" news not alone in the cities where he spoke, but even in countries which he did not touch. The important literary magazines in some cases devoted entire issues to him and the popular periodicals kept him constantly before their public. His addresses in Buenos Aires were exhaustively covered by La Nación, La Prensa, Crítica, and other papers of the capital, and these résumés were copied by the provincial press of Argentina and by the leading papers of practically all the South American capitals. Even the provincial press followed his activities, so that it is accurate to say that after his first successes in Buenos Aires, he had the attention of the entire Continent—an event never equalled before.

The following selection of critical essays has been made as representative as possible. All shades of opinion, from Communist to Catholic, are included. The purpose has been to give the reader not alone a picture of Waldo Frank's reception, but as well a sense of the temper and mind of the peoples who received him.

Romance a Waldo Frank

Fernández Moreno

Norteamericano
de claro mirar,
huésped admirable,
dulce Waldo Frank,
¿cómo tan menudo,
cómo tan cordial,
cómo tan sencillo
y tan familiar,
cómo tan violeta,
cómo tan cristal?
¿No es todo en tu tierra
torre y tempestad?

Que no eres de hierro,
bien que lo sé ya:
más de cuatro veces
te he visto temblar
y empequeñecerte
cuando vas a hablar,
cuando, ante la mesa
y el público afán,
te sientes nervioso,
te vuelves a alzar
o te sirves agua
sin necesidad,
o al reloj de oro
tornas a observar
como rostro amigo
en quién confiar.

Ahora que es verano
se podría andar

43

por esos suburbios
de nuestra ciudad,
y entre viejas tapias
de ladrillo y cal,
oro de retamas,
sangre de rosal,
ordenar el caos
del mundo actüal,
mientras el crepúsculo
se disuelve en paz.
Pero yo me quedo,
pero tu te vas.

Te vas como siempre,
por tierra y por mar,
con tu traje pardo
que es casi un sayal,
con tu cuello grande
como tu bondad,
heroico minero,
vate, capitán,
te vas en la busca
de un reino ideal
donde ya florece
otra humanidad.
Lo hallaremos todos,
dulce Waldo Frank:
tú eres espolique
en la obscuridad.

*Poem read by its author at ban-
quet given to Waldo Frank by the
contributors of Nosotros, in Buenos Aires. Published in Nosotros, Buenos Aires, in Caras y
Caretas, Buenos Aires, and in
Social, Habana.*

A. THE LEADER IN AMERICAN RELATIONS

1

THE PROMISE OF THE NORTH

What should be the position of the dissatisfied minorities of Hispano-America toward the unadapted groups of the North? To define this position would be—if we were to consider decisive the attitude of those who wage war against their time—like having at hand a vast plan for the spiritual reconquest of the continent.

Do we know in Havana the aspirations of the *exiles* found in New York? Do we realize here at all in Cuba the true reality sought by the best minds of North America? Have the more far-seeing watches of Buenos Aires, of Lima, of Quito, sighted the possibility of a practical gesture toward contact with the best of Chicago, of San Francisco, of Boston? And would any other deed merit more persistent effort and more generous yielding than this one of stretching forth a hand toward that foreign America?

Almost everything is as yet to be tried on this shore of the Atlantic—almost everything

that issues from the spirit and goes toward it.
A disciplined and alert curiosity, a thing different from the constant lustre of the South and
from the ironic gaze of the North, remains as
yet to be produced in America. We look at,
and impassioned we lament, the advance of
hostile forces. We have rarely studied with
serenity the causes of these forces; never the
distant allies whose impulse at the start of
their career, was to annihilate these anti-
human forces.

To the myopia of the South, there corresponds in the North an absolute ignorance of
things *Latin-American*. The study—at least
the observation—of the Hispano-American
phenomenon has not been made by the best
eyes, but by those interested in the maintenance
and preservation of the status quo. When
some powerful and clear-sighted eyes saw us at
close range, we became the object of romantic
sympathy. Never were we seen as neighbors
in the same world, as men called—sentenced—
to a common destiny.

There have existed—in fact, there exist—
powerful reasons for this radical isolation.
Aside from distance and language, the circumstances of Hispano-American life have
been so dramatic that in wishing to control
the course of winds which surround us, we
forget the atmospheric currents in the dis-

tance. The mistrust which the imperialistic
action of the Yankees implanted in us hindered
us from inquiring whether there was anything
more in their country than capitalistic claws.
The noise of their fabulous industries deafened
our ears to the protests of those who spoke the
truth. A time came when the over-simplified
explanations from over there and from here,
assigned virtues and talents on the basis of
the color of men's hair. All understanding—
aside from the emptiness and impenetrability
of the Foreign Offices—seemed impossible.
America was divided into two distinct and
contrary and hermetic worlds.

The last germs of Romanticism and of
Bohemia have been latent in our writers and
artists without these victims even knowing it.
The reign of the vague and of the pathetic
confined artist and writer to a shut world,
removing them from realities both immediate
and distant.

A superior vision, hesitantly formulated,
seems to mark there a new political program.
Happily, there is in process of integration
across the old frontiers an attitude essentially
human. Already a complete joining of the
younger forces is not deemed impossible. It
seems that one can hope for the weakening of
the monster by the archers who surround its
lair.

But the desire for continental action will be worth nothing if, as formerly, the contact is sporadic and the information incomplete; if everything melts into a new romantic current; if we do not make a direct examination of opposed temperaments; if the roads to be traversed are not studied immediately; if the lances which together we must thrust into the wounded flesh of the existing order are not chosen in time.

Let us, without false shyness, show our wounds to those people in the United States who are worthy and capable of showing us what is corroding their gigantic machinery, and who fervently desire to remove the infected parts. Let us ask the Northern minorities to reveal the basis of their dissatisfaction and their concrete plans. And let us challenge the direct observation of their fields of activity. Men like Waldo Frank—to whom is dedicated the greater part of this number of our magazine —can, through the uprightness of their word and the greatness of their art, tell the dissenters in their country the measure of our tragedy, and force them to say *their word* to South America.

Editorial, Revista de Avance, Habana

2

THE AMERICAN IDEAL

As has often been said, the proximity of
nations cannot and will not be realized except
through mutual understanding. To understand is to love and both, being capacities of
the spirit, can only be realized by the spirit.

The time has come when commercial and
industrial relations should be developed and
diplomatic missions reinforced and strength-
ened. Neither will, however, bring about
mutual understanding. The former, on account of their material basis, affect only the
business world; the latter, strictly speaking,
being of a nature that concerns governments
only, do not go beyond the sphere of matters
purely official.

It behooves the shoulders of large-minded
individuals to constitute themselves ambassa-
dors of peoples. It is they who, while convey-
ing to us in person their message, try to plumb
our depths that we may reveal ourselves to
them. Their action is reciprocal. On the
one hand, they give us their truth, and on the
other, they seek ours. And if happily those
large-minded individuals find themselves on a
very high plane, above and beyond the plane
which through the idiosyncrasy of their people,

we are led to suppose them to occupy; if they work and fight, fired by a high ideal of humanity which looks not exclusively at national interests nor in an exclusive manner adheres to race prejudices, then the task of comprehension and love that they bring about turns out so much more fruitful in itself that by its beauty and nobility there stirs within us a profound and heartfelt sympathy.

Such is the case of Waldo Frank, the North American writer and journalist. The cycle of lectures which he has just concluded at our National University had the virtue of attracting the attention of the Mexican public, thus distinguishing itself as an absolutely uncommon event.

Waldo Frank came to tell us his truth, clearly, candidly and undisguisedly. While expressing his thought, he spoke in the most unrestrained fashion, always guided by his foresight and his honest critical spirit. He did not recognize any restrictions in giving forth adverse judgments regarding his own country not did he refrain from evincing the same loyal frankness in reference to Hispano-Americans.

Was it by chance, or was it not, that we have now heard in Mexico for the first time the word of an Anglo-Saxon philosopher so free of Anglo-Saxon prejudices? For the fact is that Frank, through his thought, is free of all

racial prejudices.   It is not without point that
he belongs to that group known in his own
country as the "intellectual dissenters," those
men and women who have detached themselves from the common tendencies and who
affirm the necessity of attaining progress toward nobler horizons by roads diverging from
the usual and traversed ones.

In the series of lectures which he delivered so
brilliantly, Frank affirmed the following thesis:
that in the New World there will grow up a
newer world; that America, because of the
peculiarities of its situation and history, because of many other involved causes, is destined
to be the crucible of a new civilization.

We do not attempt, nor would it be possible
in an editorial, to evoke for the reader the
personality of the lecturer during the development of his thesis.   Nor would it even be
possible to abridge the essential features of his
lectures.   Frank, in his devotion to the new
and great America which is in process of being
formed, offends old Europe by being extremely
depreciatory of her.   The decadence of the old
world does not seem to us to begin with our
modern epoch nor in that epoch during which
Western civilization reached its maximum
splendor; nor precisely has the latter died, so
that London or Paris can be compared (as
Frank compared them) with marts of extinct

5

civilizations like Teotihuacan or Benares. We
live within the frame of European civilization,
the people of the United States as well as the
rest of the continent. And yet, neither in our
own nation, nor in any other nation, can be
perceived the preliminary splendors of that
magnificence that might come to substitute it.
Still it is far from us to proffer a detailed
examination of Frank's doctrine. We only
want to point out something which is included
in the splendid exposition of his thought, something which is summed up in an idea, that,
were it to take root in America, would give us
the basis of our continental greatness.

The North American thinker—an individual
truly uncommon in this Yankee period of the
world—has made a fundamental criticism of
the North American ideal, the upshot of which
is *comfort* and the attainment of wealth. He
thinks that this ideal, guided entirely by the
material satisfactions arising out of the pursuit
of power, is in want of soul. He recognizes
that capitalism, in the grip of which the world
finds itself at present, is simply the transitional
point between the old and the new eras.
Imperialistic capitalism—affirms Frank—is not
creative but is rather destructive. It will
promote, and in fact is promoting already, the
improvement of the material medium in which
man develops himself. But the invading harm-

ful forces of industrial capitalism must be opposed by the people in which that capitalism has its source and power, and no less by the weak and threatened nations.

For such a struggle, it behooves the North American minorities to generate a purely human ideal, an aspiration for the wholeness of life, right in their very land where people think only of the multiplication and satisfaction of power. But what is the duty of the Hispano-American nations toward the threats of capitalistic imperialism? First of all—and we are simply voicing the idea already expressed by Frank—in the measure that these nations are economically and politically strong, they must affirm their nationality and nationalism by working fullheartedly for integration within their boundaries.

He who has expressed himself as Waldo Frank did, nobly, disinterestedly, with wide-awake eyes, ever eager to surpass the actual, scrutinizing the present for the improvement of the future, is no longer the friend of one people; but something more—the friend of *peoples*. As we in Mexico, so the rest of America, will listen to Waldo Frank with deep sympathy. His truth is, when everything is said and done, our truth.

Editorial, El Universal, Mexico

3

North American Reaction
to Our Problem

Waldo Frank, our cultured North American visitor, has had the unusual generosity of telling the truth at the home of his hosts, in the lecture course which he has given at the National University. Contrary to what we Latin-Americans generally believe, all the problems which affect our domestic life are conscientiously being studied in the United States; and Mr. Frank is a representative of this group of men, qualified because of his impartiality to suggest fundamental points of view needed in all true political science.

In his last lecture, Mr. Frank spoke of the "Unborn America" and of the material, however chaotic, from which in time may rise a superior civilization. With the serenity and conscience of an expert he deals with matters which we have considered well-known; but his expression and vision of our problems, above all, his sincerity, lend a warm optimism to his proposals and move us to make a few commentaries.

While speaking of the industrial infiltration —the one real force of the so-called North American imperialism—and which he declares to be "a constant presence in Mexico," Mr.

Frank points out distinctly the source not only of all political equivocations but also of the fundamental errors among us.

Modern civilization is distinguished from the ancient ones by its emphasis on economics; if other cultures were able to give to posterity intellectual and moral examples, ours must proceed in an inverse manner, creating first the sources of economic stability and then projecting superior forces for the future, but always with regard to the vital interests of society. Therefore, with admirable judgment, Mr. Frank tells us "that we need to know ourselves as Mexicans and as men." The statement is justified. The North Americans "discovered themselves" and from this discovery they gained their strength. Their originality in action was revealed in an admirable ability to adapt to present conditions without prejudices or bonds of the past; and in this way, with concentrated conscious energy, they have amazed the whole world and come to dominate, economically, almost all the Powers.

We Hispano-Americans have not wished to awaken to the great and urgent reality, embodied in the social instinct. Our individualism, product of our old disciplines of solitude and isolation, is incompatible with the present Era. The economic weakness of our Indo-Hispanic nationality is the effect of that microscopic and somewhat romantic individualism; and is being continually manifested in all our problems. In order to live, in order to do more than vegetate, we must create for ourselves not only agricultural tools and industrial resources, but also capital, which if it comes from outside binds the governments of America and corrupts public opinion with negation and stagnation.

Much of what we call American Imperialism is the product of unpaid debts and of unfulfilled party promises. The only way to be free of these party promises, as Mr. Frank sees it, is to make use of the technique of modern progress and thus obtain a unity of economic purpose. No fatality has befallen us, except the inertia inherited from the crossing of bloods and of ideological prejudices—factors which are no more than an excuse for appearing so grotesquely before history.

This spirit of real discipline, which we, according to Mr. Frank, should extend to our internal affairs, will enable us to progress and instill in ourselves a true national spirit. All nations impoverished by internal difficulties have an unhealthy expansion of politics converted into an art; while those nations with prosperity and order, keep well in the background the quarrels of (more or less) significant personalities and thus succeed in making politics a pretext for general progress.

The wise advice of Mr. Frank is timely; and we are not surprised that it is voiced by a foreign representative who has succeeded in seeing better than ourselves the real source of national salvation. Our writers on international affairs have not been able, in spite of their abilities, to come to any practical conclusions regarding this matter; on the contrary, their labor has come to naught through sterile criticisms and all has ended in the "Words, Words" of Hamlet.

One culture facing another culture: such is the recommendation of Mr. Frank. We shall realize this, only when, stimulated by the North American example and by the understanding of our misfortunes, we release the energy of theories into the energy of deeds. Let it be said once for all: American supremacy is a proof of efficiency, a moral lesson; and this supremacy has come to be imperialistic, only through the clandestine concessions of many of our American governments, which behave, before the world, as individual entities rather than as agents of public progress.

Editorial, Excelsior, Mexico

4

Priest of Truth

BY

Francisco Ichaso

He is mistaken who considers Waldo Frank's visit to these Americas one of courtesy or flattery. This would be to lend it the aspect of President Hoover's mellifluous tournée—an interchange of diplomatic genuflections, or that of those banquets which Hispanity and Latinity organize to "make America."

If Frank's interest in our people were in the slightest degree a mockery of these "isms" of international courtesy which have selected our countries as a provident field of cultivation and pasture; if his intention were to flirt with our republics (so susceptible, it must be admitted, to the least gesture of adulation), it would have been easy for him to exploit the ingenuous belief, widely circulated hereabout, that he is an American renegade, a deserter, one who in the struggle of North against South has placed himself decisively on the side of the South which, it may be supposed, is the side of Justice.

Clearly, Waldo Frank has not done this. He is not (as the guardians of the commonplace

Yankee principle might well have imagined) a strange abortion out of the belly (grosso modo) of the Northern Republic; his ideas indeed have firm roots in the fertile and authoritative minorities of his country. Still less is he one of those who consider the new world as ineluctibly split into two halves: the bad to the north, the good to the south, the exploiters above, the exploited below. This absolute method of division, which still has many followers in suffering America, continues to be disastrous for our own growth. It constantly moves us to play the role of victim in the American drama, a role which in principle is scarcely tolerable but which in the end adapts itself so well to our turn of mind that we embrace it complacently and even with a certain gratuitous and barren pride. Therefrom we derive a feeling of "capitis diminutio," an organized "consciousness of defeat" which succeeds in stamping itself as glory whereas it is a seal of inferiority.

We have been inclined to overlook the true Americanism in Frank, to forget how readily he has always replied whenever his patriotism was offended or placed in a doubtful light. Recently, we were reading his reply in *El Sol*, of Madrid, to certain rather superficial strictures of Ramón Pérez de Ayala on the United States. In this rectification, we find the up-

right American who recognises the chaos of his
country, admits its vices and limitations; but
who calls for a certain purity of vision in
contemplation of the virginity of his land's
forces—forces which may yet lead deluded man
to a new historic turning. To this concept of
the potentiality of peoples, abused today by
the atomic transitory struggle of our economic
order, we must refer the whole Frankian system of thought and of aesthetic; similarly, he
projects from his vision of old Spain a fresh
energy for the creating of a new world in the
two Americas.

If the message of Frank has any flattering
balm for our America, it is not so much that he
recognises our possibilities and has faith in
them, as that he reveals the deeply human
failure of a civilisation with which we have
been unable to compete—not because we have
lacked desire to do so, but for want of that
will-to-power, of that dynamic action which
are the secret of North American greatness.
But to regard Frank as the "anti-Yankee,"
the sentimental Hispanophile, the foster brother
of the type of Spanish American who with
complacent masochism plays the role of victim
(the while grieving that he cannot change
places with the wolf), is to form a very inadequate picture of the author of *Our America*.

I am told that in a certain private talk,

Waldo Frank, when quizzed about the problem
of our relations, classified the Hispano-American
countries in two groups: "those which have
suffered too much and those which have suffered too little." In the former, the hatred of
the Yankee is a defensive attitude and wholly
justified. In the latter, the hate is resentment
and envy. The Yankee hegemony is feared,
but hypocritically this emotion hides behind a
false sentiment of Spanish American solidarity.
Thus, an anti-Nordic mechanism is fostered,
together with a subterranean, slightly childish,
imperialistic longing.

There are many among us Hispano-Americans who would love to be the fishers in these
potentially agitated waters which, alas! never
become quite stormy enough. They pretend
to admit the "natural law" of Yankee authority down to the fourteenth parallel; and would
then create a kind of "super-nation" from all
the lands to the south. Thus, actually, they
are replying to North American imperialism
with a pseudo-imperialism of their own—one,
indeed, that is quite typical of the nations that
have produced so many virulent dictators.

Waldo Frank did not come—and in this, he
cheated primary Hispano-Americanism—to
flatter such sentiments, or to align himself with
any hatred in the shock of North and South.
He came to bring us the sincerity of a message

that is painful to his countrymen who lead maimed and factitious lives, but that is painful no less to ourselves who still bask in the Epoch of Emancipation and permit the dreams of past glories and dim hopes to cradle them. For the evil of America—so tragic to Frank—is not the evil of North America alone. It is no exception, in the world of today. Differences are but of degree. In one of his Buenos Aires lectures, Frank made this plain: "The human drama of North America," he said, "is not exclusively American; it is the universal drama of our time. It is the drama of a period of transition; the drama of the hour which intervenes between the death and the birth of a world." And then, "The American vices are the universal vices of an age in which the old spiritual and cultural bonds have broken and man is naked—like an atom—dissolved from the Whole of which he must once more form a part."

The America, then, whose vices Frank discusses, is a *total* America, one integrated by geographic and economic reasons, and, most important of all, by *destiny of birth* in the world of tomorrow. Arraigning his America, he does not absolve ours. Nor is there any reason why he should. What effective measures have we taken against the expansiveness of the North? Have we before this menace behaved

ourselves austerely? Have we not perhaps
consciously and unconsciously helped to exac-
erbate its predatory instinct? Are we not
gambling with American capitalism, compro-
mising with its obscene demands in mere
exchange for the bolstering-up of our own small
and miserable capitalist existence? And our
governments, what are they doing? Serving
the interests of American capital, abusing
public wealth, violating individual rights.
Where should we look to find the vigorous
strengthening of our own nature?—the one
force that we can bring to bear against an
invasion that is spiritual as well as political
and economic.

With good cause could Waldo Frank say
in this same lecture—given in Mexico and
Bolivia as well as in Argentina:

"To the South of my America, in Mexico,
in Nicaragua, in Cuba, in Panamá, false values
from the North grow and grow, because the
true values inherent to these lands have lost
their vigor. If it were not that in the Central
American countries, those who foster these
false values—which it is so easy to call American—are men of position, these values would
never have come in." And then, replying
with grave and dramatic words to the belated
Arielists [1] who no longer convince anyone, he

[1] A reference to the enormously popular *Ariel* of Rodó—a
Uruguayan author who simplified the problem by calling Hispano-
America "Ariel" and North America "Caliban."

says: "Let Spanish America look at the Caliban within herself; the Caliban which collaborates so gladly with the Caliban of the North. . . ."

This is scarcely flattering to our ears. The hour was ripe for a priest of truth to sober our gluttons of complacency. The man of North America, neglected at home because he espouses the unrealized ideal of Roger Williams, of Whitman, of Emerson, of Thoreau, and of Lincoln—of all those indeed whom he rightly calls his spiritual fathers, sees our hands raised in clamorous suit for justice, but sees that these hands are not all clean. There are even those who have an understanding with the men who feed—and devour them. The Calibans of North and South are brothers.

The evil, then, is general. It infects both halves of the one body. It has more virulence, without doubt, in the North, than in the South. And this means that with us it has met more organic resistance—it does not mean that with us it must be less efficiently combated. Frank, indeed, acknowledges that we are more "intact"—more healthy. Our inferior coefficient of civilisation helps to save us. To paraphrase a metaphor which he uses in *The Rediscovery*, our "Jungle" is closer to the ecstatic jungle of the Amazon than to the electric machine-infested jungle of the North. Our "jungle," like the aboriginal, still nurtures man who may have faith in it, since with the exception of a few known plants and brutes, it leaves him in peace. But the North Americans are the hunted of their "Jungle"—and they feed it.

Definitively (and this is the synthesis of Frank's thought concerning the urgent problem of relations between the two Americas)— both of us must find freedom through a single threshold. Today, it is the eye of a needle through which only the alert minority may pass. Tomorrow, a broad opening on a pristine landscape. . . .

Revista de Avance, Habana

5

Itinerary of Waldo Frank

BY

José Carlos Mariátegui

Contrary to my custom I wish to begin this
article with an autobiographical note. It is
four years since I published my first impression
of Waldo Frank. At that time, I had read only
two of his books, *Our America* and *Rahab*, and
a few articles and stories. This South American echo of his work would not have come to
Frank's notice without the intervention of a
writer who has already disappeared: Adalberto
Varallanos. Frank received a few lines from
Varallanos, together with the "Boletín Bibli-
ográfico de la Universidad" (of San Marcos)
where my paper appeared; and he responded
with cordial thanks. Thus began our relationship; and from then till now, Frank's claims
to my admiration have increased. Everything
of his which has reached me I have read with
the intensest interest. But what has brought
him closest to me has been a certain similarity
in our directions and in our life-experience.
The intimate, personal reason for my affection
for Waldo Frank lies in the fact that in part
we have followed the same path. This article,

which is my welcome, will not speak of the
intellectual differences between us; its theme,
spontaneous and sincere, will be our brotherhood. For Waldo Frank is for me an older
brother.

Like him, I felt myself American only when
I went to Europe. In the paths of Europe, I
encountered the America which I had left
behind me and in which I had ever felt myself
absent and strange. Europe revealed to me
to what degree I belonged to a primitive and
chaotic world, and at the same time urged me
to the duty of an American task. Nevertheless, for a long time after my return, I still
had no clear sense of what that task must be.
I knew that Europe, when it had conquered me
entire, had returned me to America and Peru;
but I had not yet analysed this reintegration.
It was in 1926, when I read in *Europe*, the
Parisian monthly, the beautiful pages where
Frank explains the function of Europe in his
own discovery of America, that I began to find
light on my own case.

Frank's adolescence in New York had been
an enchanted revery of Europe. The mother
of the future writer was a musician. Beetho-
ven, Wagner, Schubert, Wolf, were the familiar
spirits of his household. Possibly from this
musical version of his world was born Frank's
way of conceiving of his books as symphonies.

6

The paternal library was another stopping place in his American evasion. The adolescent Frank questioned the philosophers of Germany and Greece, more intimately than the poets of England. When he went to Europe as a boy, he met familiar landscapes. His older brother frustrated his plan to study in the University of Heidelberg, "condemning" him to Yale. Finally, freed from daily journalism in New York, Frank found the Europe of his dreams, principally in Paris. He was overwhelmed by the cordiality of its reception. Paris, "city of the fortunate, of trees and gardens, indulger of all liberties and humors," offered to the young man who had changed his dollars into francs a most placid and comfortable life. For the young artist of cosmopolitan culture, the refined metropolis was home.

But the sap of America was thick in Waldo Frank. This ease in Europe could not satisfy his emotional balance and his creative power. "I was happy," wrote Frank, "but I was not *necessary*. I fed on what others, through the centuries, had created. I lived as a parasite." In these words, profoundly and terribly precise, *I was not necessary*, Frank articulates the spirit of the *émigré* whom Europe cannot hold. To fulfill his energy, to achieve his life, a man must feel himself necessary. The American who is more than a spiritual leech of the refinements of

Europe will discover himself in Paris, Berlin, Rome, an exile—and an embryon. The more deeply he possesses Europe, the more he subtly assimilates its essence, the more imperiously will he find his duty and his destiny to be to create, in the chaos of the new world, what the Europeans of antiquity, of medievalism, and of the Renaissance inspire us to fulfill. Europe herself, in disciplining the creative stranger for his work, expels him. Decadent and tired, she is still rigorous enough to demand of each man his own appointed task. Europe is bored by outlandish rhapsodies on her own thought and art. She demands of us, above all, the realization of ourselves.

On his return, at twenty-three, Waldo Frank begins his true work, under the influence of this profound experience. "With all my might," he says, "I went to work to find for myself a place in a world that seemed to be getting on very well without me." When, years later, he returned to Europe, America was already born in him. He was already strong enough for the audacious scenes of his voyage to Spain. Europe had already acclaimed him as the poet of *Our America*, as the novelist of *City Block* and *Rahab*. He was in love with his deep enterprise; with magnificent spirit he could cry: "We may fail, but even so we shall succeed." This time, when he took ship for New York, Europe was "left behind."

It is impossible to feel the implications of this experience of Frank, unless one has somewhat shared it. Europe, for the American and the Asiatic, is not alone a menace of denationalisation and uprooting; even more, it is the best means for recuperation, for discovery of one's destiny and self. Not every *émigré* is fatally a *déraciné*. For a long time, the discovery of the new world will be a journey on which one embarks from a port of the old continent. Waldo Frank has the passion and vitality of the North American; yet, as I say of myself in my book on Peru, in Europe he performed the best apprenticeship. Would his sensibility and his culture be so modern, if they were not European? Were not Whitman and Poe better understood in Paris than in New York, in those days when the young Frank asked himself who were his nation's representative men? French Unanimism went to school to Whitman in an epoch when America had yet to conquer her great poet.

There is another epoch in Frank's formation, which my own experience helps me to understand: his journalism. Journalism may be an excellent training for the thinker and artist. Someone has said that many a novelist and poet, sneering at the journalist even as the old men of the theater mocked the cinema, would fail lamentably as a reporter. For the artist who knows how to free himself in time, newspaper work is a laboratory in which he may develop critical faculties which otherwise might remain blunted. Journalism is a sort of speed-test.

I shall close this orderless and subjective disquisition with a journalist's question: even as it was a Jew who, in the Victorian epoch, alone felt in all its magnificence and with the luxurious fantasy of the Oriental, the Imperial rôle of Britain, may it not be reserved to this Jew—in this cosmopolitan age—to formulate the hope and ideal of America?

Variedades, Lima, Peru

6

Presentation of Waldo Frank

(*Before the Instituto Hispano-Cubano de Cultura of Havana*)

BY

JORGE MAÑACH

In offering to you the three lectures of Waldo Frank, whom you are going to hear today, tomorrow and the day after tomorrow, the Instituto Hispano-Cubano de Cultura feels that it is serving, in a distinguished way, the aims that gave it life, and therefore the finest, and the most urgent, cultural needs of Cuba.

This invitation extended to the eminent North American writer is in a way an exception to the usual practice of our Institution. To be sure, this is not the first time that our platform has been honored by a non-Hispanic speaker. But this is, I believe, the first time that our guest—twice guest since he is foreign—makes no professional claim in his mastery of our Hispano-American culture. Mr. Frank has no contact with the political chancelleries; he is neither diplomat nor professor. In fact, he might be called "anti-professor," and "anti-diplomat." For the first time, we have gone to the North American world for our guest, having regard only for the universal nature of his message.

I am going to take the liberty to say that this invitation—determined by no Hispanic sympathies—amply fulfills the spirit and program of our Institution. I shall say it concretely: every time that there exist in any foreigner the three essential qualifications of Waldo Frank—his excellence, his accessibility and his appositeness—the Instituto will do its best to bring him to this platform. For mind you, our name is not "Instituto de Cultura Hispano-Cubana," but "Instituto Hispano-Cubano de Cultura." They are not the same. The adjective refers to our constituency: the name "cultura" is free and unshackled, as culture must be.

It would be simple to justify Waldo Frank's appearance on this platform by reminding those of you who are Spaniards that this is the author of a book replete with the splendors and gallantries of Spain; and by reminding those of you who are Cubans that this is the North American most assuredly with the deepest sympathy and understanding of our half of the Americas. Spain has had few exegetes so lovingly devoted to her significance; and we few friends so zealous of our dignity, so watchful of our fate.

But the truth is that if we have insisted that

Frank visit us at the end of his journey through
Mexico, Argentina, Chile, Bolivia, Peru, it has
been less because of the gratitude we feel for
him already, than for that which we hope some
day to owe him. We are in the presence of
one of the truly solitary spirits of the world—
one of the richest and most versatile in North
America. He is a thinker who extends horizons, he is a critic who analyses not simple
forms, but substance itself; he is a novelist
powerful and compassionate—a man of such
voluminous and diverse strengths that there
are not yet years enough, nor perspectives
enough, to measure his height and to assay
the atmosphere in which he lives.

It is true: the perspective is not yet ours;
yet already we can sense the distant splendors
of his vision, even as we can see that the North
America which he envisages is less luminous
and less triumphant than the one which we
ordinarily picture.

In the United States, his voice is one of
dissent and prophecy—an "apocalyptic" voice,
to use his own descriptive adjective. His
task is that of the leading agent of a new
cultural-critical philosophy in a country until
now singularly confident in the substantiality
of its powers and of its modes of living. It is
Frank's intention to reveal from this platform,
as he has done on so many others, the precise

nature of his disconformity. My duty is
merely to point out to you the significance
which this young man assumes for us, who,
challenging the superlative delusions of the
world, has joined the sacrificial company of
those who tell their people the whole truth—
the whole dolorous truth.

There is a tale of Waldo Frank's, about a man
who, having gone out to buy his wife a Christ-
mas present, yields to the solicitations of a
bibulous friend, gets drunk, squanders his
money, and returns to his house with neither
gift nor the wherewithal to buy it. What will
he say to the good woman waiting for him?
The sinner resolves to tell her the truth.
"Let her know" he says. "Let her see clear.
This will be my present to my wife. That
she may see clear, and be free."

This admirable episode seems to me to
symbolise the ethic of the writer Waldo Frank,
—his heroic, liberating, dynamic sense of the
truth. His two great works of cultural criticism: *Our America* and *The Rediscovery of
America* are formidable inquests, not in the
tone of nihilist invective, but in the spirit of
one who seeks foundations for building a
better house, and cannot avoid sounding the
ominous gaps that underlie the surface. Waldo
Frank has discovered these gaping voids in his
own country, because he wishes it to "see

clear and be free." Thus, our great guest
brings us an example of his truth—seemingly
so cruel, really so full of love—the truth which
we have not yet organised in our own intellectual life, having but theoretically accepted it;
"the truth" which, as Don José de la Luz has
put it, "can alone clothe us in the toga of
manhood."

The substance of Waldo Frank's message
is of peculiar importance to ourselves. It
would be vain for us to conceal the fact that
in the naturally imitative infancy of our
people, we have, while forming the modes of
our individual and collective life, excessively
patterned ourselves after the great Northern
patron, which, indeed, has almost succeeded
in imposing its ways upon the world. And,
what is worse: we have taken from North
America not its best side of democratic intent,
but those excrescences which Frank has called
the "cults of Power" and which threaten to
destroy its own creative and organic virtue.

Let us not be misled in hearing Waldo
Frank's animadversions upon his own country.
Already, he has pointed out to us, in one of his
lectures in Argentina, that we also have within
us, in common with the United States, the
factors of our own destruction, and of our own
sterility. Cuba, through its proximity to the
North, and through the mediation of the

North's contagious will in all orders of our life, needs more than any other of our nations, the light of criticism upon the false and the real values of the United States. We need to learn, from this minority American, that all that shines is not gold or rather, that what shines is indeed too often gold.

On the other hand, we offer to Waldo Frank —man of the intelligent left (which is to say, not of the blind and simplistic barricade), the chance to study in ourselves the effect of the exercise of that cult of Power which his country is practising on the weaker nations of America. The spirit of the pioneer, so admirably studied by Mr. Frank, is not dead. Mr. Frank knows that this spirit has simply exhausted its opportunities at home, and is now spreading across the nearby seas. And he knows that this new manifestation of the pioneering spirit lacks the "inner check" which tradition gave it in its earlier stages. It moves, naked of ethical scruples; its affirmation is the bare urge of instinct.

Yet, if in these lands of ours the instinct of Power has found allies of a similar nature, the minority which today so jubilantly welcomes the free word of Waldo Frank wars against these common foes—at home or abroad, fighting without truce but with hope. We also aspire to be a people with that "beginning consciousness of self, intense, homogeneous, separate, absolute, which is called race." We believe that in spite of geography and economics, our history and our will give us this right. And we believe that your message and your testimony, Waldo Frank, will help us and will vindicate our hope.

In making you welcome to our free platform, we beg of you that you tell us also the whole truth. For we are learning to face our truth, in order "to see clear and to be free."

Excelsior, Habana

7

The Visit of Waldo Frank

BY

Julio Jiménez Rueda

Waldo Frank has been, for the past month, the guest of the University of Mexico. He has given a series of lectures which have awakened unusual interest in all those who are concerned in the evolution of our America. The ideas of his lectures are virtually those expounded in his most recent book: *The Rediscovery of America*, published this year in English and now in process of translation into the Castilian. Set forth before a Spanish-American audience, they have, however, deeper because more intimate resonance; and to the original stock of ideas others have been added that give a vital density to his subject. For, arising from the profound traditions of North America, they grapple prophetically with the ideal of a new race—a race that struggles to deserve its name by creating the New World baptised by the discoverers.

To Waldo Frank, modern Europe is a chaos, but Asia and America are a chaos also. With the break of the political and religious unity of the Middle Ages, there arise multiple tendencies in life, which are but fragments of the world in dissolution. The Middle Ages were like an organism perfectly coordinated at least in theory; a machine; and men and institutions only wheels of this machine. With the Renaissance, the machine broke, and hurled its sections into every direction; and no modern synthesis has as yet regathered them together.

Individualism, romanticism, humanism, communism—none of these has sufficed to embody the form of the New World which all men seek. The history of North America, ideologically, is the history of the quest of the new form for this new world, which—at last—must come. But when? Years, lustra, centuries, perhaps, will pass before it appears, finally, to bring peace to man who from the heroic times of the discoverers, and through the lives of explorers, warriors, statesmen, poets, has dreamed of its coming. All those who have meditated on the American future have contributed to this search for the American ideal. Minorities keep on weaving the amazing warp of this ideal into the space and time of history. Its light shines, if indirectly, on all lives. Men and women, black and white, grope *en masse* toward this light as toward a North star. And the ideal, crossing the frontiers, ceases to be North American, and becomes continental.

The dissolution of the old world is manifested chiefly through the separatistic cult of "power"—a power that is expressed through money or through comfort. The American lusts to increase his possibilities of comfort, sacrificing thereto even that which justifies or motivates comfort—his home. And the American woman does not find in her man a true lover. Whence, for Frank, the rise of the rebellious "flapper."

From the pure explanation of the North American scene, Frank passes to a study of the relationship between the two Americas. A common enemy: Capitalism—in all its psychological and cultural ramifications. A common means of action: dynamic knowledge through the intelligence and mutual understanding of minorities. Across the spaces of our Americas, moves the salutation of those who have a single message for mankind.

Contemporáneos, Mexico

8

Waldo Frank and the Two Americas

BY

Félix Lizaso

"Only America is a good word, and
prophetically it covers us all." *W. F.*

1

Above all else, Waldo Frank claims for himself the quality of artist. His interpretations
of America, of Spain, are those of a great
constructor of syntheses who illumines his
visions with mystic fire. He says to us:
"I see no basic difference between the art of
relating characters and that of creating concepts to explain the life of peoples." His
books, therefore, are very far indeed from the
tracts, over-brimmed with precise data, which,
lacking spiritual breath, pretend to explain
life's pattern through external facts. In Waldo
Frank, the great abstractions—arduously ob-
jectified at times—open underground highways
which suddenly grow light and lead us to the
very heart of problems. At times, the artist
lingers long over an idea which he is explaining
to himself as if to make his own position clear;

we forget for a moment the thread we have
been carrying; but when, once more, we strike
the trail, the road is more open, leads more
directly to a final integration. That sense of
the Whole on which he dwells so passionately
in *The Rediscovery*—is it not the very essence
of his method? Waldo Frank is a man possessed by the sense of the Whole. Were he
not a very great artist, his work would not
achieve the symphonic plenitude which is its
nature and which gives a kind of apostolic
life to his message.

2

A philosophy of the whole cannot but be
conciliatory. Modern science dislodges God
from "the field of reality," and puts Nature
in his place. But falsehood does not lie with
the latter, nor truth with the former. "The
number of compartments in Hell is important,
if you believe in Hell; even as the number of
electrons in an atom is important if you believe
in the atom." Wherein lies the difference
between the two sciences—theological and
natural? At bottom, it is the difference
between what is bounded and what is boundless—between the Mediterranean and the
Atlantic. A new Sea brings us a new dimension, that of boundlessness. And what is
boundless in man is his action—his will.

7

Europe in a way realised her wholeness. The maximum of verticality and height plots the maximum of perfection. A centripetal force brings about cohesion on the shores of the small "middle sea" where huddle the people of Europe, thus completing the cycle of Mediterannean culture. Now, at a certain moment, a rival force—centrifugal—presses these people to search for a new sea and a new world. Americas appears at this symbolic hour, to affirm the will which endows America with life. The expression of the will replaces, in philosophy, the "Unmoved Mover" conceived by Aristotle and apotheosised by the ideal of the medieval world: an immobile Christian status.

America is the result of a disintegration. She came to being, spiritually speaking, in fragments—not as the transplantation of the Whole of Europe; hence, the isolated forces which invaded our America were of a distinct nature from those of the other America. The whole of Europe was integrated by the most heterogeneous components imaginable; when these components once again recovered their respective characteristics, as a reaction they accentuated their separateness.

The loss of the spiritual sense of life brings along very diverse reactions in the man of America, who like Perez de Ayala's Prometheus, comes into the world with an old and shapeless soul. Excess will always be his law, because he lacks the sense of the whole. He will be a growth of isolated incomplete forces: materialistic excesses, religious excesses, moral excesses, political excesses mark him. That is the law of America. Conquering, however, that confused period which made us believe ourselves superior beings, on the strength of our *Latinity* and idealism, or made them believe themselves superior, on the strength of their practicality and their power,—we arrive at the new insight which begins to tell us that the materialism of the North is not worse than the materialism of the South. Cariolano Alberini's words during his masterful presentation of Waldo Frank in Buenos Aires shed a great deal of light: "At any rate all of America is materialistic. Ours is the materialism of sensibility, theirs, the other America's, is the materialism of the will."

The materialism of the will finds its formula of equilibrium and its *raison d'être* in the conquest of power and comfort. We do not clearly know towards what formula this materialism of our sensibility is headed. Yet it seems to us that sensualism, the opposite of effort (sensualism and weakness clasp hands) is at the cross roads of all our highways. Let us recognize the fact that at this hour many

minds wish for no other thing than to shed
light on the most genuine motives of American
behavior and to direct them, if feasible, toward
the Utopia of America.

Each one of the two Americas, in a thorough-
going manner, has been busy crossing these
roads which the expansive force inherent in
their being assigned to them, and those roads
in each hemisphere had to diverge. But while
the North was moving to its overlordship of
power at an accelerative speed, deaf to all
voices which might retard her from reaching
her goal; our America has not stopped dreaming
of a brotherhood of all peoples, linked by love
and understanding: the very opposite of the
Monroeism of the North. And it is Frank
himself who, facing us, writes these words:
"Hispano-America will be a symphony of
voices, from Mexico to Tierra del Fuego; for
the variety of their ethos is great and, in Plato's
sense, they have the music." But we are
bound to admit it: it has not been up to the
present more than mere dreaming: at times
an attitude but never a determined purpose.

Did America, in reality, mark the birth of a
new world, or on the contrary, turn out to be
the grave of an old and decadent race? Which-
ever of the two formulas we pounce upon, if
taken singly, would lead us into error. No
conception could explain America with more

felicity than Waldo Frank's. Very well then:
Can America fulfill her whole as did Europe?
Only by becoming a symphony. It is the
most generous dream that an American can
possess, especially an American of the North.

That explains why Waldo Frank has now for
some time been heeding the call of our America.
His message to the intellectuals of Hispano-
America in 1924 was a promise and it was
already a friendly voice. "My message is
very simple"—he said at that time, "and it is
that we must be friends. Not friends of the
ceremonious kind, of official acts; but friends
in ideas, friends in acts, friends in a common
and creative intelligence. We have the obligation to carry out a solemn and magnificent
undertaking. We have the same ideal: to
justify America, creating in America a spiritual
culture. And we have the same enemy,
materialism, imperialism, the barren pragmatism of the modern world." But at the time
he wrote these words and when he later wrote
those words in *The Re-discovery of America*,
Waldo Frank did not know us except through
the virginal essence of Spain and through the
writers and artists of our lands, who had begun
to broaden his vision. Later he told how he
suddenly felt the need of knowing us. Did his
recent contact with our lands confirm him in
his conclusions? Did it reward him for his

arduous search of America? And finally,
did this contact strengthen in him the belief
in the necessity of American Unity?

He will learn that in our America as in his,
we live in an epoch in which the spirit has not
yet spoken. But perhaps he might have to
change an idea of his, as when he points to
the possibility of a union of Hispano-America
and his America; provided the latter, going
against the grain of her practical tradition,
follows her mystical tradition, ceasing thereby
to be the blind force that she is at present, in
order to change into the symphonic nation of
his dreams. At this juncture, he assigns to
the America of the north the first move to be
taken, while he gives to ours the rôle of re-
sponding to her call. But did not Frank himself recognize that, in opposition to "the sick-
ness of power," which it is just to call Americanization, our America has a profound sentiment of her destiny and the strength of her
mystical tradition? We happen to be much
nearer the fundamentals of his conception;
it will be much easier for us to effect the integration of our dreams than for them to get rid
of their worship of power and comfort.

The *approchement*, no matter how it is
brought about, must somehow be attempted;
but independently of each other, each America
must acquire her spiritual flexibility; if possible

at the same temperature, so that some day that continental brotherhood can come into being and be the conversion of the American world into a whole.

Waldo Frank is not a simple theorist who paints, in dark colors, catastrophes and chaos; he is a creator of values, who brings us his formula for salvation. The evil of America lay in the fact that the fragments of a whole which reached a perfection in the past, "survived severally, energized by the illusion of being separably a whole." Hence there is in the last analysis one evil, the lack of the sense of the whole, no matter what has been the road traversed in pursuit of deceptive fragmentary images. And the cure ought to be beneficial to us in the same manner. "We know what we need: men who will act as conscious integers of the whole and who will thereby create it: create, in this America of ours, the paradigm of the world."

It has always been said that America has unsuspected reserves: with these reserves she can construct her whole. Her experiences have been almost solely external, she has not said her word, harassed by the growing necessities at her very door. Frequently she has been blamed for her mistakes, an easier thing to do than to illuminate the road. The great uselessness of many of our prophets is traceable to their taking the present facts as alarming manifestations, spreading a panic without localizing or checking it. The superior task would be to forge unity.

In opposition to the values in currency, which tend to maintain the false standards that rule us, no way is open other than to create the new values of human significance, which having their start in the individual acquire strength and solidarity in the group, the true reintegrator of the American whole which we all must aspire to. This method of Frank for bringing into existence the whole, ought to have validity for all: we must reach the whole by means of the group, whose essence is to be found in the man capable of sensing within himself the finality of the world.

Where, but in America, can the future of the world be born? America is the threshold: "the future of the world is the future of the American fact." In order that America may be wholly realised—America which is now reduced to fragments by its political constitution, it will be necessary to substitute Frank's beautiful concept of the symphonic nation with that of symphonic America. Our share in this claims us. A crowning idea can bring the miracle into being.

Revista de Avance, Habana

9

AN INTELLECTUAL EVENT IN BUENOS AIRES

BY

José María Salaverría

Through Buenos Aires have passed the most enlightened lecturers of the world. The great intellectuals of Europe were wont to speak to the Argentinians if not as mature persons to younger ones, at least as outsiders. But recently the North American writer Waldo Frank has put a stop to that practice. He has spoken to the Argentinians as from within; that is to say, he has placed himself in the attitude of the American who speaks on equal terms with other Americans, and who speaks to them, moreover, about the destiny, responsibility, and spiritual mission of America, in relation to the emergent problem of a new world culture.

This happy thought of the great North American writer has received its deserved reward. Although the public of Buenos Aires is accustomed to manifest lavishly its goodwill and its applause to all the notable representatives of the mind who reach its shore, toward Waldo Frank its applause has gone the limit, to such a point that it goes beyond all that has been known up to now. We can well be permitted to call it an exception; or we may even use the word *record*, since we are dealing with something genuinely American.

In order to register the degree of enthusiasm which this fact has produced, suffice it to say that Señora Victoria Ocampo, the most active exponent of the feminine intellect in the country of the Rio de La Plata, putting aside her favorites Rabindranath Tagore, Ortega y Gasset, and Count Keyserling, is preparing to go to the United States to found a review of great import, for the purpose of gathering and expounding the thought of all America.

We find ourselves, then, before an event of extraordinary interest. America begins to demand an autonomous place, a place distinguishing her from the rest of the world. America begins to wish for a conscience, a continental personality, not, strictly speaking, in the political or economic sense, but in the realm of intelligence, spirit, and culture. And this type of separatism, like almost all separatisms, assumes the form of protest against the incapacity of the conqueror and a will to develop freely one's own possibilities for genius. Indeed, the flattering effect that such an attitude may have on an impressionable people can readily be understood. Waldo Frank has told the Americans of the South that Europe is a thing in crisis, a continent crumbling with old age; and that in the dramatic moment for assuming responsibilities, it is the duty of America to extirpate from its own soul all vestiges of Europe's dissolution, in order to create for herself a new culture, and be born to a new and individual life.

Were we to lend an ear to wagging tongues, we might suspect that the great North American writer has really not done more than collaborate in the campaign of propaganda which the United States wages in order to retain its practical control of all America. The fact is that Waldo Frank has done more for the United States than all the high personages who, up to the present, have visited these countries on missions of *rapprochement*. This should serve to help enlighten those torpid minds who believe that a writer is nothing but a simple expounder of amusing and idle phrases. Even in terms of advertising values, an intellectual can be considerably more successful than all the advertising offices of propaganda in New York or Los Angeles. That is what, in fact, has occured in the case of Waldo Frank.

Waldo Frank began by presenting himself in a manner very different from what the majority expected of a Yankee specimen. Nothing of bigness, broad shoulders, vigorous

gestures, and strenuous ideas; the Argentinian
public, on the contrary, saw appearing before
them a medium-sized man, rather timid, of an
insinuating voice, who spoke to them in a kind
of mystical intonation, somewhat like an augur
or seer. The Hebrew blood in Waldo Frank
must have helped undoubtedly to produce
that effect. All the meaning of the catas-
trophic ideology of Spengler is, on the other
hand, to be found in the writings of Waldo
Frank, who does nothing else but utilize in an
American fashion the Spenglerian idea; that is
to say, he begins by affirming that Western
civilization is virtually moribund, but forth-
with he wishes that America attend to her
own affairs, that she should separate herself
from Europe, that she should seek salvation
by herself. To attain this purpose, he addresses the Americans of the South with a
prophetic air, kind, suggestive, impressive,
and captivating. It was in this guise that
Buenos Aires saw him.

The creation of the New World needs both
Americas: he has told the Americans of the
South. He continued to add: "There exist
minority groups in the United States dedicated
to our task. In no other country is there more
goodwill, more talent than in those minority
groups of the America of the North. In no
other country is there a similar group more

beleaguered with danger. For the enemy is upon us. Every force in the United States is centrifugal: on the surface of our lives there is light, success, money. The North American of talent must needs be heroic in his will in order to resist the corruptive force of success, in order to remain obscure, a quiet focus of American life whence creation comes forth. The North American creator needs help. Our position is precarious. The food that we receive from the brilliant, swooning-away Europe more often than not is poison rather than food. Let us betake ourselves to you. In many ways you are more intact. . . ."

It is easy to understand the effect these words have had on the Argentinians. Let us imagine, for a moment, the effect which they must have had on a Leopoldo Lugones. Accustomed as the Americans of the South are to the great minds of Europe who consider them as people in the process of becoming, as pupils to be taught, and in truth as colonials, the fact that an eminent mind grants them full equality has overwhelmed them with righteous joy. The North American writer has touched the most sensitive fibres of South American pride. He has asked of them nothing short of their spiritual collaboration for a common task. He has said to them:

"With us you share America, the dream,

and the ideal, and the mission of the New World. With us you share the common threat, a false world organism, organized by Power and for Power, a creator of chaos. On our behalf I beg you: grow more conscious of yourselves, more articulate. Control the wealth of your energy, formulate your vision. The task of creating the values of the new world needs each and every one of the nations of both Americas. . . ."

Very well, then: there is in America a secret and hidden separatistic movement which cropped out in the very distant days of the first colonization, and Waldo Frank has now become its clear spokesman. He speaks without beating about the bush of the mission and spirit of America, opposed to those of Europe. It is, in short, an undisguised public declaration of American separatism. Does there exist in reality a separate continental mission? Can America really make by herself a new gesture? an autonomous culture? It is not easy to answer a certain type of question. On the other hand, it is indisputable for whoever knows in its intimacy the American soul, that there exists in America a continental spirit, vague and hidden at the same time, but capable of manifesting itself with force when the occasion arises. To the old type of nationalism there will be the need, then, to add, soon, perhaps a new form of separatism: continentalism.

The question whether in America can be formed a very strong continental conscience, a kind of Panamerican patriotism, is one which, because of its transcendental import, exceeds the bounds of this article. Perhaps all that Waldo Frank has said in Buenos Aires may not be more than the plaything of a professional mind which practices its trade as it travels. But I believe that these questions have a real significance, a true interest for everybody (for the Spaniards they should have an interest more than for any one else); and with the view of giving information, I have here set them down.

A. B. C., Madrid

B. THE THINKER

10

Signposts to the World of Waldo Frank

BY

Jorge Mañach

All ambitious thinking starts from the hypothesis that there is order in reality and that this order is capable of being reproduced in concepts by that class of ideation which we call logic. Knowledge then is understood as a conjunction, the thoroughness of which depends upon the plenitude and ambition of our capacity to speculate.

This principle of conjunction is the great concept of the *a priori*, the initial and unprovable condition of all thinking. The true problem of knowledge is not to verify this hypothesis—without which we would remain in a desperate situation—but given the possibility of a correspondence between the order of concepts and the order of reality, to test this relationship, to establish its certainty.

It is well known that no one has come in closer proximity of this proof than that reached by Descartes: that the true thing is

the clear thing. Unfortunately we do not
discover the reason why it is impossible that
error should not present itself to us, also
clothed in resplendent brightness. So then,
what can brightness itself be but the suasive
halo of strong logical cohesion? And how
many diverse and adverse so-called "truths"
do not dispute our assent, armed as they are
with dialectics? To pretend to find the mark
of our ideal coincidence with things in that
criterion of greater or less clarity, i.e., logicality,
in the version that we have of them, is to
ramble about in that vicious circle of an epis-
temology which says philosophically, "I can
have my pie and eat it."

Strictly speaking, every thinker, who like
Waldo Frank seeks the whole, dogmatizes his
pristine position. The affirmation of cosmic
harmony does not go beyond being the affirmation of unity found in thought, and its substantiation is only the evidence of a robust
ideational capacity. There is no reason for
declaring that things are not a chaos outside
of the fact that it is unpleasant for us to
think them chaotically. That is to say: not to
think them at all. As a monster of curiosity,
man does not resign himself to not giving
himself some version of reality, and as he can
only reason out a coherent version, he conceives the world as something that has order.

The universe is an explainable matter; to what extent, depends on the capacity of the explainer and this capacity is not only a question of logic but also of adhering with love to ideas and having confidence in their reality. Granted this transference of the conditions, proper to thinking, to the cosmos, we can readily understand that philosophical ambitions should tend to postulate a world as unified as thought itself, as hierarchical and harmonious as the most careful game of syllogisms. Only that thinker who is a pluralist, at bottom an impatient creature or a skeptic, can reject an explanation of the whole. Being a future hunter of truth, he goes swiftly past philosophical landmarks, picking up his game in a careless manner against all the decrees and prohibitions of logic.

Because these men do not appeal to the eloquence of their architecture nor to that of their reasoning, but to a more brutal resource: a lyrical and rhetorical capturing of conviction, a violent contagion of enthusiasm.

II

If Waldo Frank intrigues us so much as a thinker, it is because in his integral architecture, in his complete version of reality, he combines powerfully the two methods: the logical and the impressionistic, the classical and the romantic. His dialectic is a close weave of reasoning and rapture, of syllogism and image, of analysis and emphasis. The "frozen mountain tops" of reason sparkle in his work, with the effulgence of an Apocalypse. Mounted on a spirited Pegasus, he jumps heedlessly over the ravines of thought, perhaps less through a lack of precaution than through his greed for new perspectives. He is a great critic, illuminated by poetry. Possibly he has been led to this frame of mind by the astute, conciliatory sense and the vigilant vehemence of his race which has the knack of giving the right turn to its phrases accompanied with exaggerated gestures. And above all we find in him the felicitous union of the creative artist (he is a master of synthesis) with the critic (he is a master of analysis). The first gift enables him to make vibrantly plastic his most subtle abstractions and to love them as real, human, close-at-hand things; the second gift endows him with the patience almost of the anatomist, and with an appraising and divining sense. His rationalism, then, is drenched in lyrical essences, in vital juices, as if at last Poe's and Emerson's constellations had crossed each other's path on the American firmament.

In fact there appears to be no doubt at all of Frank's right to the rank of eminent thinkers.

He exhibits spontaneously the mark of the
genuine thinker: that rare capacity for penetrating to the light of things. It is not
equivalent to having mere insight or mere
lucidity. There are writers gifted with a
sustained perspicacity and with extreme clarity
when it comes to rare instances of ideation but
whom we cannot rank as first-class thinkers.
In reality they are nothing more than writers of
subtle or sharp or suggestive thoughts. But
the aristocratic quality of thought manifests
itself in breadth as well as in depth. To
sustain in equilibrium, as it were, a large and
powerful chain of ideas is worthy of a mental
athlete's prowess. The true thinker is, consequently, the man who does not have to write in
order to be one; he can sink back in his arm-
chair or hide his chin in the hollow of his hand
and discern at a distance a whole family or a
whole hierarchy of ideas. He has the observ-
ing glance which discovers in every apical
concept its most hidden beats and its most delicate ramifications. In this is founded the
current notion that the philosopher is most
exact and most true when he expresses himself
completely in an all-inclusive system. But
it is clear that he is not a philosopher because
he is systematic but rather in spite of that.

The outstanding trait of that capacity for
getting at the inside of things is the power of

anticipation so evident in Frank. However empirical his prejudices may be, the true thinker reveals himself to us and to himself, as a thinker of the *a priori*—as a man capable of formulating general ideas previous to any rational experience. Immersed in his work, he is the master of the arena who knows what is going to happen and heralds it without qualms to the logician who is not prepared for it. It will be said that in a book this is a question of technique, of outline, of architecture. But in philosophy the plan in itself is already an elevation. The sheer beauty of architecture worthy of a cathedral, in a work like *The Rediscovery of America*, offers much more than a dialectical abundance, hand in hand with aesthetic sentiments; it reveals rather what Waldo Frank insists upon so much: *vision;* or what perhaps amounts to the same thing, a plastic sense for abstractions.

The other quality whereby the philosophical rank of the American thinker is determined is that quality to which I have already alluded, the virtue of intellectual love, the capacity for becoming fond of one's own ideas. Perhaps dilettantes and skeptics are what they are for lack of the emotion which makes of the speculative occupation an aesthetic and most vital experience. Strictly speaking, there are not, nor have there ever been philosophers of

skepticism, for that presupposes a distrust of
reality and of the vital efficacy of ideas. It is
necessary to believe in their fertility in order to
risk that great betrothal and concatenation
of ideas, which is, after all, what we mean by
a system. Possibly modern thought has lost,
—with so many other innocent traits of candor
and loyalty,—this faith in, and devotion to,
ideas. Perhaps because of a vicious habit of
absolute factualism traceable to Positivism,
because of a lingering distrust after the seeming
failure of the centuries-old contests among
systems, or because of a caution before the
vacillations of science, the background of
modern thought is, if not skeptical, at least
extremely suspicious. For this reason, and
there is no doubt of the matter, philosophers
aspiring to integration are not to be found
aplenty. But the enlighteners of fragments
are with us. Also the great industry of thinking has been given the vertical dimension.

The emphatic exception that he represents in
this sense confers particular interest on Waldo
Frank's preoccupation with the whole. Certainly in the United States where even pure
thought is always offered in segments and in
a pragmatic fashion, the example of Waldo
Frank has few equals. Our memory at this
moment does not recollect any other case
than Santayana's. Intellectually, Santayana

is not an American. It is not less true that
intellectually speaking Waldo Frank also is
not an American. This would explain his
harmony with the thought and sensibility
of the Mediterranean culture. But this is a
delicate question. Under the pretext of ex-
amining American culture, the author of
The Rediscovery of America has sketched for us
nothing short of a metaphysical and moral
system. That many facets of his system have
been noticed to be partial and not a few obscure
in their implications, does not detract from its
all-embracing intention, nor does its importance
in any way suffer on that score.

III

Wherein lies this importance may be asked.
Certainly not in the conception of the Whole.
This idea is of very noble ancestry. From
the Upanishads to Spinoza, (Frank himself
reminds us) the human mind has demonstrated
that there can be but one true substance. The
validity or conclusive efficacy of this demon-
stration has been combated by all the modern
forms of agnosticism and skepticism. The
war waged in the nineteenth century against
metaphysics left behind the burning-hot em-
bers of prejudices against all forms of the
gnostic absolute; and in the United States this
suspicion was encouraged by that over-acute

pruriency in favor of facts which is so characteristic of the genius of that country. Under
these circumstances, to found a criticism
implacably hostile to the Narcissistic American
culture, on a metaphysical concept such as
the Frankian sense of the Whole, was to face
bravely the reproach of mysticism, which
Frank has displayed proudly as an emblem.
Because previously Bergson left a gaping
breach in the Positivistic and rationalistic
ramparts, it is not a whit less impressive to
see the boldness with which this neo-American
has rushed to the very stronghold of "atomism"
to place his mystic's pennant.

In support of the principle of monism, he
contributes, with that energetic eloquence of
his style, new dialectical resources founded on
certain modern agreements, such as the subjective origin of the religious feeling and the
binding sense of the aesthetic experience.
But what matters definitely to Frank at the
moment is not so much the establishment of
an ontology but the application to the theory
of culture of a metaphysical principle, saving it
thus from that coarse empiricism of the
pragmatists and from the deterministic pre-
suppositions held by such men as Spengler.
He wishes to restore to the concept of culture
the significance found in a work of consciousness and in the religious deed.

To this end, even the application of the
principle of the One to behavior is not something
new with him.   The central ethical idea is the
same as that of Spinoza who in his turn had
already a vigorous antecedent in the Stoic
morality: the idea that the perfect life is only
possible when lived in conscious rapport with
a universal meaning, with a cosmic will.   But
the critical use made of this standard assumes
in Frank's latest work a vigor and an intensity
seldom equalled.   The undertaking was the
more arduous in that Frank tried to apply a
metaphysical criticism not merely to the
generic moral life but to the ethical and
cultural phases of American life, which—for
all their unanimity—are enormously diverse.
The penetration and cohesion which Frank
achieves in his diagnosis of the evils of the
North, traceable as they are to a will both
particularistic and "atomistic," is a great
event in philosophical criticism.

Definitely, his action is chiefly on the ethics
of the individual.   As so many thinkers from
Socrates to Bergson, Frank knows the error of
pursuing the absolute outside of ourselves and
seeks it in the experience that comes from
within.   Inspired by the great exhortation of
the Jew from Amsterdam, that we all live
sub specie aeternitatis, Frank believes that the
discord between instinct and the harmonious

will of the whole must resolve itself by the
individual's imaginative power, by the adop-
tion of new images, that should put into movement our behavior and maintain it always true
to its "verb" function and not to its "noun"
function in the syntax of the world.   To be sure
this functional consciousness is for the present
given to us in a very dim fashion; we hardly
have more than an intimation of it, for only an
antecedent comes to mind.   We find it in
Buddhism, where contemplation is purely mechanical, and in the ineffable Bergsonian
"duration."   But it is not difficult to see in
this idea the germ of an ethical methodology
having great possibilities.   At last an American
methodology may be possible.   Frank may
turn out to be the inventor of a true technique
of behavior, a system whereby the mystical
experiences of man may become a real matter
in every-day life.

IV

It is clear that a thought so compressed and
so novel cannot but leave unexplained some
controversial points.   The initial concept of
the whole, so earnestly postulated, is perhaps
no more than a suggestive logical embryo, as I
pointed out in the beginning.   There may
still be cause to say here in some measure what
Hegel said of Spinoza's Absolute: "a lair of

wild beasts to which all tracks lead but from whence none return." Upon what depends the cosmic will? What justifies its imperious pretense? How is it possible that there be discrepancies and individual rebellions against so sovereign a vocation? Who assures us that Power—begetter of so many odious cults—is not the most loyal expression of the creative will, as Nietszche thought?

Perhaps Frank wants, and is in the position, to dissipate such doubts in those books still to come, which he has promised us. And if not, it does not matter. Doubt is the inevitable shadow that concepts project before truth. And finally it is not so necessary that concepts be demonstrated, as it is that certain convictions be formulated. Those of Waldo Frank have illuminated a critique that is probably the most valid and surely the most brilliant and profound that has ever been made of American life, the image and pattern of modern existence.

Revista de Avance, Habana

11

INTRODUCTION TO WALDO FRANK

(On his Reception by the National University of San Marcos, Lima, Peru, as Doctor Honoris Causa)

BY

LUIS ALBERTO SÁNCHEZ

Professor of American Literature in the University of

San Marcos

Will Waldo Frank forgive me, if I break the forms of friendship forged between us during his brief stay in Lima, in order to discuss him as a professor of the *Faculdad de Letras*, on this occasion of his reception?   I do not know. But I do know that he has profoundly understood the meaning of this ceremony, and that he appreciates the act of the Faculty in inviting him to speak from this tribunal and in offering him the honorary degree of Doctor.   And I know, moreover, that he is able to assay the union, this morning, of the austere, centuries-old tradition of our University, with the faith—millenial, since it is rooted in the Prophets—yet eager and youthful of Waldo Frank.

I undertake this introduction, not so much

through the texts as through the personality,
the feeling, and the rhythm of his entire work.

1. Message

It is in the Old Testament prophets—the
first message-bearers—that one must seek the
emotive accent with which, despite his elegance, Waldo Frank speaks of the universe.
Of the universe and, by inverse gradation, of
America, of his country, of his generation, of
himself. His message is his own experience.
But this experience adumbrates until it is a
cosmic one, so that his "I" merges with the
whole, and his America becomes the intimate
living of every man who knows himself and
feels his duty and his function. Thus it was
that in his first lecture in Lima, "My Message
to Peru," Frank could say in all simplicity
that the title of his talk concealed a Yankee
trick, since his message was in reality himself—
his person and his life.

The meaning of this "trick" leads us to
consider the American message. We have
suffered from a plague of messages. Everyone
who has felt himself called (self-called, as
likely as not) to discuss the general affairs of
America has referred to his "message." And
usually the message turned out to be a churchly
pastoral or a military proclamation, although
they who launched it called themselves laymen.

The message, indeed, is a kind of commercial *poster* for ideas.

Against this class of message, Waldo Frank reacts. It is not his fault that his essentially critical genius undergoes the inevitable tension of his race, whose impulse is most visible in Isaiah. Because of this, his criticism has the emotive note to which I have referred. This criticism, human and profoundly moving, is his message. It is a message that states enough, exhorts little, integrates much, and raises criticism into a system of harmonious construction, deeply illumined by its own analysis, in place of the usual critical method of dissociation and allusion. When a man's message is his own life, his own experience, synthetic, harmonious, and deeply illumined by self-analysis, then the counsel and example which emerge from it will also be harmonious, profound and creative. Every synthesis presumes the indication of a rhythm. Rhythm, then, is another of the characteristic traits of Waldo Frank. And his message is essentialized in that discovery of himself, one day, in Europe which brought as its immediate fruit his lucid understanding of American reality.

2. *The Tragic Sense*

Waldo Frank is more widely known through his interpretive works than through his novels.

Among the former, *Salvos*—an admirable collection of aesthetic studies—is usually neglected. Among the latter, the best known are *Rahab* and *Holiday*. The public, as well as the author, has a way of forgetting *The Unwelcome Man* (1917). But it is waking up to the existence of the stories in *City Block*.

The novels of Waldo Frank—the part of his work which he loves most—reveal a tragic, mystic and transcendant sense of life and literature. *Rahab*, with its Hebrew title, gives us a woman sinner utterly distinct from the sinners of French novels—a sinner with a supernatural *pathos* and *fatum*. Among the most beautiful pages in *Holiday* are those that describe the mysticism of the Negro: in the church, all pray and proclaim their infinite anguish; in the lynching party, all rhythmically move against the hunted black, not to deliver him to justice but to vent their own hate and passion.

There is no coolness in these novels. In them, woman's love touches the category of the transcendental, the supernatural: in them, the agony of the Negro is transformed from the picturesque to the semi-divine, by virtue of being so profoundly human. There is a similar intensity of life in the tales of *City Block:* and something of the same to be found (with a far different technique) in the *Manhattan Transfer* of John Dos Passos who also, like Frank, is of Jewish origin.

The problem of literature, for Frank, is a manifestation of life. He is very far from the current literary sportsmanship of Europe. He disagrees with Ortega y Gasset's "dehumanisation of art"; he is in accord with Unamuno when he writes: "Nothing has wreaked more havoc with true spirituality and the true sense of religion than the aesthetic obsession. Æstheticism has poisoned the religious wells of the so-called Latin nations."

Literature, thus, recaptures its human category, despite the pure literary style, and the clear rhythm, of Waldo Frank. For him, the man who prehends the truth in its wholeness is the one real artist; and *rhythm* is not the result of the professional skill of the writer, but the product of an integral organization of thought and feeling, before expression.

3. Interpreter

His use of rhythm—integration and counterpoint—and of a kind of plastic transfiguration in the form of symbols, gives a peculiar accent to the Frankian interpretation. His interpretive works are four, but only three exist in Spanish: *Our America* (1919), *Virgin Spain* (1926), and *The Rediscovery of America* (1929). These three books are feats of rhythmic creation. Waldo Frank has an amazing gift for traveling: he seems to need no guide.

What he does in life—plunge into the streets of an unknown town, burrow through its obscurest alleys, find his own direction, test and search everything, in silence and alone— is revealed in these books. Thus, in *Our America*, he employs the most variable means for his synthesis. Politicians, dancers, business-men, writers, pioneers, cowboys, artists, churches, public squares, cinemas, sports, newspapers, merge into his symphony. This word is one that especially pleases Frank. He applies it to his *Virgin Spain*. Violoncellist in his youth, and profoundly musical, he composes his symphonies in rhythms of music. It is only a man musically gifted who can essentialise totality from such diverse matters.

Throughout these works, the interpretation rests upon the necessity of integrating, of making *one*, and above all of sustaining the rhythm. This indubitably is a method that has its metaphysical, its mystic sense: a sense that is clearly Jewish.

4. Integration

From the dance of Spain, together with a number of detailed, seemingly independent facts, the intuition of Waldo Frank distils a system and a synthesis. From the chaotic life of North America, he constructs a panorama. He alligns diverse, even contradictory

9

elements. A politician of the type of Bryan, one like Wilson, a man like Debs, the artist Stieglitz, the dancer Duncan, the writer Mencken, the star Chaplin, the playwright O'Neill, the flapper, jazz, the life of Hollywood, the traffic of Chicago, the frenzy of New York, the face of Dreiser, the racketeer Capone, President Hoover: and with all that, like one creating a world, he expresses his single central thought, its synthesis, its totality. And he has done this because he has been able to detect the unitary rhythm which underlies phenomena and persons seemingly—only seemingly—so discordant.

With Spain, he does the same. He observes the dancers of North Africa, the Andalusian woman (as admirably pictured as the flapper of New York), the polemicist Unamuno, the Cid, the poet Valle Inclán, the *torero* Belmont, Juan Ramón Jiménez, Quixote, the Castillian, the plain of Castille, the type of Isabella, the nostalgia of Columbus; and from this motley mass rises the magnificent symphony of *Virgin Spain*; its main rhythms and motifs leading without difficulty to the organized totality of the author's vision.

Waldo Frank avows that he is going to try to create a synthesis of South America, for he feels dimly the unitary rhythm of our life. But he does not venture to sketch so much as a chapter of his book, for he still lacks its basic idea—harmony, panorama, rhythm. While this is wanting, it is impossible for him to plan a work, with mere intellectual elements of union. The rhythm which Waldo Frank needs is, then, not a rhythm that is ideated or imagined, but a rhythm that is *felt*. He has to experience his work, before he can plan it; to perceive the intimate harmony of his whole; by an effort of the intuition to penetrate to the essence of his creations. Then, and then only, the intelligence intervenes, to order, shape and discipline the central movement.

Nothing could be finer than his jazz-interpretation of American life. Jazz, as the expression of submission, plaint and protest—saxophone and banjo—bespeaks the sentiment of the North American minorities, and the obscure anxiety of the majorities, trammeled in the machine, whose subconscious will yearns tragically to be free of industrialism and the inhuman, absorbing, dangerous Imperialism of their country.

The Jew speaks in Frank, with incomparable force. He seeks the world, in the man. His New World, that which he announces, is nothing but this self-illumination and this self-experience. Nor is his Jew one who mumbles in the synagogue or has a peculiar cast of feature, or Sephardic ancestors, or who desires

to pilgrimage to the Weeping Wall and spill
his blood there, if need be, for the rebirth of the
Hebraic nation. The Jew of Frank is the man
with Jewish ideas. It is the idea which integrates, since the idea is a *form* of spirit. Race
is a lie, if there be no race of ideas. The
Jew is the archetype of all minorities. And
every minority man has something in common
with the Jew.

5. *The Problem*

Frank insists—and who does not?—that
there exists in North and South America an
urgent problem. A problem which demands
an urgent solution. The ultimate generations
of our Continents are above all involved in this
solution, since it is they who have had to face the
bitter problem of surviving—of acting in order
spiritually to survive. But to solve this problem of America, there is a sole first step: to
understand it. This implies a profound analysis. Analysis does not come to all who wish it;
it calls for capacity; it calls for *objectivity* in the
analyst. And objectivity itself entails a critical function of the highest order.

Nevertheless, Waldo Frank arrives at his
synthesis by intuition, and in the search for
the truth, he accords first place to the artist.
Only the artist can apprehend the truth. Art
and truth come together through intuition,
and are resolved into a pure *subjectivity*.

By this way of intuition, subjectivity and art on the one hand, analysis, criticism, objectivity on the other, Frank elaborates his thought. When certain critics have seen in him and his work the tendency to make the Americas homogeneous, he has always replied: "No: I want harmony, integration, cooperation between the Americas; but identification would be suicide. Each part of America must conserve and evolve its individual traits." We must not forget that there is a page in *Virgin Spain* where these words are written: "Jewish internationalism is a subtle poison." Naught is more unitary than human individuality: and only by this path can one attain the unity of the World.

6. *Romanticism and Discipline*

Within the fatigue of the industrial and materialistic world, Frank seeks living founts, sources of renewal for his whole and human hunger. Thus, he writes of California, takes pleasure in the original rusticity of Bryan, wanders through lands still primitive or pure, like Spain, South America, Africa. But we must not deduce from this that Frank is a Rousseauist. In Rousseau, he admires only the impulse to develop the free personality of man. He accepts only the *Emile*, yet even here there are basic differences: for Frank, the child, the primitive, is not the perfect and happy creature upon whom a malignant civilisation is imposed. The child, he has said, is sensual, savage, cruel, egotistic—very far indeed from the angel with whom he is compared. Possibly, closer to the devil. It is culture, intercourse with others, that lifts the child to the level of the human, which is to say, the divine. Very far indeed is this from Rousseau.

But there is something more. Frank preaches discipline and *method*. The most anguished problem in his country is for him the search for a method. Jazz complains and rebels, because there exists no discipline for re-creation. Chaplin suffers and stumbles, like a personification of this pathetic quest for method. In the skeptics like Mencken, in the "romantic critics," in a formidable teller of tales like Sherwood Anderson there are the same symptoms: dissatisfaction and, at the same time, helplessness, because of want of discipline and method. The whole critical movement of ten years is nothing more than the bootless search for method. Objectivity, organisation, totalisation of power, integration of disparate impulse—*method* is the great modern problem. In America, there is Revolt, protest, an enormous will for reform: but north and south, what is lacking is technology and method. That is why Frank tells us that his

message is himself and that he found himself
in Europe, for it was Europe which taught him
the painful lesson of method no less than the
proof of its own exhaustion. "Europe," he
implies in *The Rediscovery of America*, "is a
corpse." But a corpse, as Frank observes, is
not an inert body; a multitude of creatures
swarm within it. Only the dynamic method
that can make use of all these diverse lives is
wanting, therefore the body as a whole is
dead. Discipline and method are needed to
transfigure the contradictory dynamisms of
modern life, released from the old Life of
Europe. In the disoriented Rousseau, there
is no similar lesson, no such persistent defense
of method.

7. Position

And now, we may try to place Waldo Frank.
Artist and critic, creator and master: of the
artist, he possesses the indispensable need of
finding the truth, and of the critic the gift to
expound it. His race and education define
him well. He has the Jew's messianic faith,
the mystic and cosmic sense, the ability to
feel himself one with the universe and to
individualise the world or—better—to uni-
versalise the self. His education brought him
clarity, a Latin rhythm in thought and in
expression. And of the North American Pur-

itan he reveals, in ever increasing doses, two marked traits: spiritual honesty, and the stubborn will of the frontiersmen. But this battler is by no means a "struggler for life."[1] Men of this stamp, according to Frank, maimed their personality, cutting it off through a fearful egoism.

In the literatures of America, especially in those of the south, there is no parallel to Waldo Frank. Possibly, there are greater thinkers, more devoted apostles; but no upholders of systems. Our apostles always personalise in their work. Their disquiet moves them toward public affairs, but always through personal allusion or some group. Sarmiento through Rosas; Montalvo through García Moreno; Martí through Spain; Prada through the clergy. They worked by virtue of certain potent and infallible reagents. Only with Rodó do we begin to find the type of disinterested and abstract thinker. It is the same with the artists as one can understand in Prada and Montalvo; not in Sarmiento. But Rodó was a professor; he lacked scope and pace; and these mean life. He spoke for an Academy; his instances come from philosophical works; his guide was a professor of skepticism, Renan, and a professor of vital paradoxes, Guyau. Waldo Frank has an immediate vivid contact with

[1] English in the text.

life itself. His faith *acts;* his ideal becomes incarnate in a method, since potent impulses are worthless if they do not create for themselves the discipline and technology of action.

There is a phrase, bitter and terrible, in *Our America:*

"During a hundred years of her material existence, America succeeded. Success meant suppression of life: we have seen to what measure. The man who dreamed, loved, created rather than possessed, was a byword and a pariah. Life retreated—its mystery and infinite passion—to the domain of Failure. In Failure, Life dwelt and survived. In Failure, the new prophets found it. The highest singers of our day—in prose or verse or pigment—are the singers of the holiness of Failure."

But Failure imposes itself. The new man must bear in mind that "in a dying world creation is revolution." And that the artist's rôle is not to reflect or express, but "*to transfigure.*" Every creator must be a transformer, that is to say, a revolutionist. Because Failure, when exalted to a norm, ineluctibly leads to this goal, in contrast to "success" which makes for the enthronement of the separatistic ego. Waldo Frank, champion of Failure, foe of the "success" of his country, revolutionizes by creating, and enacts his function of artist, in the effort of transfiguration. It is no wonder

that they who group themselves at his side in
his own country should be few: nor that it
should be natural for Frank, when he comes to
an unknown city, to walk alone and free through
its streets, wooing its intimate rhythms.

For within the immense masses of his America, Frank appears in the same relation as when
he comes to unknown cities: *free and alone*.
He bespeaks for us a North America that is
free and alone, which is to say—a minority.
And the representative men are of use for him,
only in so far as they articulate his country's
protest and rebellion. An interesting point:
in these lectures of Waldo Frank in America
Hispana, his compatriots do not go to hear him.
There are no Yankee faces in the hall.   Neither
in Lima nor in other countries. Those that go
are his *compatriots of ideas*—components of
the great race of ideas which he proclaims.
Even in Islam, he saw chiefly an idea on the
march.   An idea that required cohesion.   Once
again, you find the same obsession for integration, for totalisation which already in *Salvos*
(1924) made him say: "The chief business of
the American literary artist and critic of those
days was therefore the launching of a call of
rally."   And these other words which explain
his concept of art and criticism, raised to the
highest human category: "We know that even
as art is far more than expression, criticism is

far more than smiles and grimaces and frowns."

In the United States, as elsewhere in the American world, thought of such quality is rebel thought, minority thought, and free. Within the world of the machine, and the chaos called civilisation, Frank seeks the deed and the feeling that are human. When his profession is asked, he answers: "man." And since they understood him as such, far from the official and materialistic aspects of his nation, the youths of Hispano-America have received him with joy; and in Spain he is admired as in France—indeed a good deal more. Nothing offends Waldo Frank more than to hear that he is considered a propagandist of the United States. For indeed, his proposal is for another United States, still in embryon, and invisible to the eyes that have been blinded by the cement, the iron rails, the oil and coal and dollars of his official state.

8. Communion

Waldo Frank, with his books and his talks, leaves with us a deeper trace than is apparent. This artist has a direction and a goal. Let it not be forgotten that the mission of the artist is to "transfigure," not to reflect or express: that creation is a "revolution": that, in short art goes far beyond a mere aesthetic play, and that finally, as Unamuno says, if pure aestheticism is the foe of the truly religious, in Frank whose deeply religious tone is clear to all who have read or heard him, it would be absurd to seek that type of "pure" art in the restricted sense of the word "beauty" which many ascribe to him.

Waldo Frank's work is a dynamic one of creation, that is to say of revolution. But his revolution is more ambitious than the others, since it aims at an insurrection of the spirit. The orthodox forms of rebellion seem to him mere sections or fragments of the one he dreams of, and works for. His New World is not the continent which Columbus discovered; it is the New Man whose appearance he proposes and whose heralds are the rebellious minorities —the idealists—of the entire world. Minorities of Hispano-America, of Spain, of the United States, of the Jews—or of the vast and half-deserted theater in which he gave his last lecture of Lima: minorities who are expressions of the nonconformity of man today, and of his need to *create*.

In his passion for synthesis and his lucid, critical illuminations, Frank performs an enormous task. He gives us a high example of disdain for the cajoleries and tricks of the popularity-seekers, and he is distinct from the other lecturers who have come to us *to give* lectures, not like Frank who has come to us *with* lectures. By his insistent refusal of the chaos of his country—Chaplin gives us the idea in a Hollywood of oil and coal—we recognize Frank as ours, and of our race; of that race which he defined so well—the race of discontent and disconformity, but, as well, of hope.

> *Letras, a Quarterly, published by the National University of San Marcos, Lima*

12

WALDO FRANK AT THE UNIVERSITY OF BUENOS AIRES

BY

CORIOLANO ALBERINI

The presence of Waldo Frank in this University, where he may speak with complete freedom, for he deserves it, is one of the most brilliant and meaningful episodes in the cultural program of the Department of Philosophy and Literature.*

We have been striving for years to create a soul for our University, which speaking in broad terms has hitherto been free of what constitutes the essence of culture: the lyrical sentiment of truth. In the very midst of so many regressive, pseudo-progressive ideas, we have tried to give birth to a university spirit free of the three dangers which beset culture: politics of any hue, professionalism, and academic stagnation.

The subjects which are studied in this house are "gloriously useless." That is the reason why our boldness becomes intenser when con-

* The official title of the Liberal Arts Department of the University of Buenos Aires in Spanish is: Facultad de Filosofía y Letras.

fronted with the common academic pragmatism
which has not any greatness even of a utilitarian
kind. Far from being an instrument of intellectual barbarism, as elsewhere, our university
reform here was a determined effort to give
culture a third dimension; for up to the present
we have not had, generally speaking, other
than professionals and politicians. There were
and there still are professionals and so-called
statesmen in the university centers. We have
more than our share of oligarchs, and dema-
gogues are always at hand. These gentlemen
are very respectful people but not for the
lecture-room of a university, where the first
places must be occupied not by them, however
distinguished they may be, but by those men
who know that the human spirit in its inex-
haustible, creative form is worth more than its
very own values and these values more than
their accidental, manifested forms. Those
militant beliefs which so much call upon liberty
and rightly so, no matter how much they be
worth, in fact, are worth less than that same
liberty which is the realm of values. Let us
then be not frightened by ideas. In any case,
we need only fear the inferior quality of the
man who advocates them, but never when it is
a question of eminent minds, no matter what
faith theirs may be. To believe the contrary
would be like maintaining that the University

must be converted into an organ of official truths. And precisely because we conceive it as one of those places where "the spirit bloweth where it listeth," the spirit must not be allowed to crystallize in any of its manifestations, however important they may be. Such is the intellectual atmosphere of this institution.

The Department of Philosophy and Literature three years ago initiated through my proposal and through my good offices, the negotiations needed to procure the presence of Waldo Frank in Buenos Aires. A short while afterwards the *Instituto Cultural Argentino-Norteamericano*, run by broadminded men endowed with executive enthusiasm, organized this visit of his. We have Waldo Frank here with us. We knew of the man and his work. That is why we have brought him here. Frank can —please allow me this innocent play on words —be true to the spirit of his surname. Let him express here whatever his mind dictates, as he might have done in 1926 during the never-to-be-forgotten conversation we had in New York.

On account of his characteristics as an artist and thinker, on account of his spirit, on account of the texture of his ideas, on account of his knowledge of Latin culture and of the Castilian language, he was among the intellectuals of the great republic of the North the most fitting to initiate the intellectual link between the United States and our country. We put into practice similar programs in connection with the great European cultures through the other foreign institutes in our country.

Why exclude the United States in our striving for the broadening of our intellectual spirit, especially when there exists such a great similarity between our two countries?

The image of North America nestling in our minds is more or less exact, but grotesquely onesided. The Argentinian attitude, and in general the Latin-American mind, as regards its judgment on North America, usually takes the form either of shoddy advertising and irrational repudiation, or of complete and naive admiration, which is none the less absurd. By and large, the people here have a not-very-complimentary envisagement of the United States. And yet this attitude does not seem to hinder anybody from enjoying the benefits of the original creations of the vitality of that great country. North America would seem to be something of this sort, an eccentric and uncouth land which scatters throughout the world the following products: statesmen specialized in the art of bringing about public happiness by means of constitutions, genuinely federal in their character; athletes somewhat too rough; immodest dancers; cacophonous

Negroes; business-men opposed to granting credit on long terms; seekers of somebody else's oil deposits; pragmatic Christianity; the electric chair; the Y. M. C. A.; the impossible Volstead Act; the K. K. K.; skyscrapers; Amazonian prowess of a prosaic sort when it is not grotesque; technological wonders; Edison and Ford; a twangy English; epic crimes; philanthropic millionaires; smooth-shaven dentists; comfort that makes for discomfort; Babylonian urbanism; moving picture actors skilled in giving eternally long kisses in the final scenes; gigantic universities; the anti-Darwinism of Tennessee; in sum, things which in most cases prove the genius-like pushing power of that people.

Any way, it is a question of taste—this virtue which, perhaps not in great abundance in the United States, is nevertheless not scarce when you consider that, besides so many prodigies in the culture of means, you find there also remarkable manifestations of the culture of ends. If the latter culture does not come up to the high standards of Europe, blame the brief history of that country; and it behooves us to ask ourselves if there is any country where in less time people have accomplished more than in North America. It possesses whatever comes out of work, what is attributable to will power. It lacks just what is the product of a

long history. In new countries the environment shapes the spirit; in old countries, the
spirit, already master of its dynamic essence,
shapes the environment. In sooth, it is rather
astonishing despite the dangers lurking in
very great wealth, that the United States must
be credited (it has been true for years) with an
artistic, scientific, and philosophical history
appreciated in Europe. Have we South Americans anything really comparable to all this?
It is just to rebel against the soulless forms of
their capitalism and against any and all the
deleterious aspects of their international politics; and such criticisms, we must not forget, not
a few of the great minds of that country make
also. But we must not confuse a nation with
its political magnates of the dollar who happen
to be in power. Overlooking their great civic
figures, is there any need for us to mention the
great cultural tradition incarnated in men like
Emerson, Hawthorne, Whitman, Thoreau, and
so many other men of the middle of the nineteenth century or of its last half? Coming to
the very door of our times, have we any men
comparable to Royce, James, Dewey, Santayana? All of them are admired in Europe and
at least known by name by the cultured public
in any country. Usually our public knows
those artists and thinkers who because of the
peculiarities of their work curry favor with the

newspapers. The noises bruited about, however, have nothing to do with the intrinsic value of an intellectual. This literate mass has not heard of names like those of Gibbs, the great physicist, of Cope and Jennings, the eminent biologists, and of so many other scholars who are great cultivators of pure science. How many in the Latin-American countries know George Santayana, an admirable philosopher of Platonic idealism, a great writer, whose prose is a model of vigorous classicism? He, too, has made his diagnosis of the United States. He set it down in his book *Character and Opinion in the United States*. Through his deep criticism made with love of the United States, Santayana is a brother to Waldo Frank.

Our injudicious admirers of North American universities believe them to be the best possible in our world. They are mistaken. We find that there circulate in them currents of uneasiness and a strong anxiety for improvement. I became aware of this discontent while I talked to the outstanding men of those universities; these universities are not utilitarian organisms, as this idea is bandied about among us, but in many of them there is an abundance of subjects, completely of a disinterested nature. This is due to the fact that there is in North America, perceivable by whosoever is capable of doing so, a profound spiritual ferment. The type of the cultured man who worries over the problem of the destiny of North America is not rare among them. It would seem as if the spiritual off-spring of Ganivet has multiplied over there. In certain sections of the American intellectual world a deep uneasiness is at work, a living dissatisfaction pregnant with possibilities. Notice, please, that in that mechanical jungle, described marvelously by Waldo Frank in his *Rediscovery of America*, there sing, in different keys, many nightingales, some in sorrow and others in hope. Waldo Frank is among those who sing in hope and no one can stop him from singing. Let us not misconstrue, then, the generous requisition which Frank makes against his country. He also is a severe critic of his country's detractors. His diagnosis does not imply a negative attitude, but an ideal of life worthy not only of his country, but also of other countries, which behave exactly the same way as the United States, although on a smaller scale, not having the same excess vitality.

Waldo Frank's philosophy of American life is founded on a metaphysic. He will explain to us in due time in his luminous prose the idea of the whole, a difficult concept indeed. Frank, lest we forget it, is above all a great artist, but he possesses a deep philosophical

sensibility. His mental modality is explained
by his theory, according to which consciousness
has its rooting in the imagination. Whence
it follows that he understands the sheer force
of the penetrative phantasy; its philosophical,
activating motive being a kind of Spinozism
with vitalistic implications. Art then fulfills
a transcendental function, since it is the plastic
word of God, of a pantheistic God; but Frank is
careful to tell us that our human individuality
is not dissolved in the intoxication with the
divine.

Let us not exaggerate, however, the Spinozism of Frank. We are dealing with a Spinoza
run through the romantic sieve of Germanic
metaphysics; whence came forth, in truth, the
North American transcendentalists such as
Emerson and his school, whence too Whitman,
whose exalting crudities imply an amorphous,
evolutionistic pantheism changed into lyrical
stuffs. Waldo Frank belongs to this spiritual
ancestry. The North American mind shows
at times the sense of profundity which it re-
ceives from its religious instinct. This metaphysical spirit, however, has never completely
died, not even during the panic, as it were, for
economic gain, found in the myths of machine
worship and the exaggerated worship of efficiency. Much is said about North American
materialism which was, as Waldo Frank puts

it, not invented by North America. Strictly
speaking, the Americanization impulse is a
European invention. The United States has
done nothing but perfect the technological
tendencies by means of its constitutional
liberty and its great will for work, very characteristic of an energetic race in touch with a
fertile and hostile land. Let us grant for a
moment that this is materialism. At any rate,
all of the Americas are materialistic. Ours is
the materialism of sensibility, the other America's materialism is that of will. Santayana
says that "the North American is an idealist
working on matter," but this will, let us hasten
to add, is expanded outwardly at the expense
of the spiritual dimension and falls at last into
a voluntarism without any meaning, and into
the monotony of ultraefficiency which has no
clear end in view. A creative forwardness, we
admit, but very chaotic. Voluntarism (or
affirmation of the will) is frequently a metaphysic among Anglo-Saxons and Germanic peoples.
But if it has the tendency to end in voluntarism, I am bold to maintain that it is a
voluntaristic materialism and as such, romanticism, even at that of a scarce value. And it
is romantic because it bears within it the idea of
creative evolution, without doubt powerful,
but in the last analysis, as Waldo Frank says,
it is the mere will for Power. The North

American philosophy of the will does work on matter as do modern physicists: it transforms it into energy and thus matter, in fact, has ceased to be matter. Where resides the evil of the civilization of the United States? Its diagnosis Frank will give us. And,—a rare thing among Iberoamericans—he will give it in the name of a philosophy where metaphysics changes into ethics and knowledge is conceived as a form of action. For our guest, human knowledge is the awareness of an immanent Divinity which manifests itself in art, which is equivalent to being the language of God, a pantheistic civil magic, thanks to which the American efforts, upon becoming conscious, will subordinate the part to the whole. Instruments will no longer be ends, the American past capable of being utilized will acquire meaning in the center of the sense of the whole. His God, being thus an immanent God, will make it possible for us all to find ourselves in the ideal of a religious program and of a life revealed in art, which art is the awareness of life. Of course these ideas might give rise to a questioning of their basis. For us, men of clear Greco-Latin minds, they may have the imprint of a very novel and grandiose haziness. But, leaving doubt aside, they are fertile. It would not be difficult to prove that the best in human progress has been done in the name of great imprecise ideas, like the forces of nature, which are not precise on account of their magnitude. The sense of profound truth vibrates continuously in Frank, preferably as a sort of metaphysical lyricism; though it cannot help being lyrical, yet it possesses militancy. Suffice it for our purpose to remember his vigorous critical sketch of Dewey's philosophy. It is a masterpiece in the art of exploring the essential spirit of such an efficacious ideology as that of the great North American philosopher, and this criticism is made in the name of a metaphysic, somewhat fluid, although of an irresistible beauty and moral enthusiasm.

The lovers of genetic doctrines starting with racial mysteries might concoct naive hypotheses, well thought out, on the origin of Frank's thought. Let us not fool ourselves. Frank is a great American indeed, just because he is so profoundly American. His philosophy, if we look into the matter seriously, although subtler and less technical and prolix than that of Dewey, turns out to be American, and it is American because it tends to reduce metaphysics to ethics. This is quite evident to those who have studied the evolution of ideas in North America. What is Dewey's pragmatism other than a Hegelianism changed into a metaphysic of efficiency, to accord with the American environment? Pragmatism reduces,

in short, theoretical reason to a practical one.
Kant was the great culprit without knowing it.
For that reason the pragmatic turn given to
the philosophy of the will (voluntarism) at its
height, in the form which plutocratic Puritanism has bestowed upon it, finds in Santayana
its Platonic critic and in Frank its romantic
critic; for after all Frank is more romantic
than he imagines himself to be. This fact is
evident to all those who do not equate Romanticism with one of its forms, for example,
with that of Rousseau. Santayana feels Being
more than Becoming: Frank, Becoming more
than Being. If we are careful, we notice that
Frank, being a great artist, enervates somewhat, without intending it, the force of pure
thought. He seems to admit no other contemplation than that of art and even this
contemplation insinuates besides a certain
workable eagerness. At bottom, and it may
be I am wrong, his symphonic pantheism implies the attitude, or at least the initiatory
stages of an attitude, which, were it to be
developed, would lead us to the lyricism of
efficiency. Be it ever so little exaggerated,
it would be changed into the efficiency of
lyricism; and this too would be very American.
Let us say it without the least vestige of malice,
we run the risk of being led to a kind of lyricism
as a form of service. We must not be too

much surprised. When an American adheres to an illusion, let us be assured that his cloud, however white it may be, is loaded with pragmatic thunderbolts. We express ourselves thus because Frank eulogizes what he calls the "apocolyptic method." This fact changed the poet into a seer of the Atlantic culture. And it is well known that seers are the poets of practicality. Let us not split hairs. The symphonic pantheism of Waldo Frank has a very beautiful trait, it posits cordiality as the essence of the Universe. That is why it is pleasant and fruitful to discuss with him, and just as Lugones a few nights ago, in a magnificent speech, promised, if the occasion presented itself, to bout with him, that he might make him emit sparks of beauty, we in our turn, promise to snatch away from him sparks of truth, which truth is also beauty, though not all beauty is truth. But it deserves to be. Let it not be forgotten that from our very hope, and from "the quality of our search, the nature of the future America will be born," and Frank is its prophet.

Sintesis, Buenos Aires

13

Waldo Frank and Marx

BY

José Carlos Mariátegui

His work proves concretely and eloquently the possibility of harmonising historical materialism with a revolutionary idealism. Waldo Frank has the positivistic method. But in his hands, the method does not become instrumentalism. It must not surprise you that in a critique of Bryan's idealism he reasons like a perfect Marxist and that in the preface to *Our America* he puts these words of Walt Whitman: " . . . the real and permanent grandeur of These States must be their Religion; Otherwise there is no real and permanent grandeur: Nor character nor life worthy the name, without Religion . . . "

In Waldo Frank, as in all great interpreters of history, intuition and method collaborate. This association produces a superior aptitude for penetrating into the profound reality of facts. Unamuno would probably modify his opinion of Marxism if he studied the spirit— not the letter—of Marxism in writers like the author of *Our America*.

Amauta, Lima

14

Waldo Frank and Spengler

BY

León Dujovne

Within recent times, in opposition to the predominant interests of the second half of the XIXth century, the curiosity of many minds has been directed towards human life, to its concrete psychological and historical reality. One could say that man after a long and tedious excursion through the physical world has returned to himself. Spurred on by his particular problems he devotes himself to the investigation of the essence of his life and the path of his own destiny. In the second half of the XIXth century a similar interest was not wholly absent from the attention of the scientists. But in this period that attention was led astray in the investigation of the psychophysiological processes of the individual, of the volatile individual arbitrarily withdrawn from the social and historic medium in which his existence unfolds itself. Stewart Chamberlin interested himself in the XIXth century. So did Daudet, who qualified it as stupid. The investigation of the different human cultures and of the various modes of being in which the life of our species manifests itself has begun to interest the thinkers of diverse classes who absolutely free themselves from the dictatorship of Darwinian evolutionism. Men are beginning to focus humanity with an autonomous cultural and historical criterion: Spengler, Keyserling and Waldo Frank set an example as prominent leaders in this movement. They are not satisfied with the mere verification of facts. They have a common interest in eschatology and in education. They are continually predicting and advising. But while Keyserling and Frank speak of "a world that is being born," Spengler takes great pains to call our attention to the death rattle of a world that is passing. Keyserling, who is of a restless disposition and an improvisor as he himself confesses, is of the three the least systematic in his work, the least organic and coherent in his ideas. His books constitute an episodic application of the thoughts of Nietzsche and Bergson. Although he is most original in his handling of details and in his observation of accidents, he hasn't a single theoretical concept that can be considered the backbone of a doctrine. Spengler's thought is universal and constructive. The combined reading of *The Decline of the West* and *Prussianism and Socialism* verifies this. There one discovers the theory of a mathematician and of a conservative politician converted to historical researches. Spengler is a German of the war, a European of a Europe in ruins. And for this reason it is interesting to compare his work with that of Waldo Frank, a son of a victorious America.

Spengler himself points out the novelty of his historical method. To his mind, history resembles Ptolemy's astronomy. He made European humanity the central point of his studies. He conceived of it as developing along a single line from the Greco-Roman antiquity to our days, and the other nations interested him only in so far as they were antecedents of his central theme. Spengler, for his part, endeavours to understand all the cultures in the light of his investigations. His analysis is not monocentric but polycentric.

Three fundamental principles governed the writing of history in the past: the definition of culture in relation to Europe, the criterion of continuity in its development, and the method of chronology in its manifestation. To this organic trinity Spengler opposes his ideas. He defines culture by means of a biological analogy. He establishes the category of coherence in place of that of continuity, and he substitutes for chronology the method of identity of meaning, of homology, of the different facts that manifest themselves in the various cultures. He works constantly with elementary notions drawn from biology, he speaks repeatedly of the birth, the growth, and the death of the cultures. These notions, which would seem to be powerless outside their proper sphere, he transposes to the very different domain of the human cultures. For no known reason, founded for the most part on insignificant details, he establishes for all the cultures an identical duration of 1000 years. The common destiny of them all has been and will be extinction after the process of decline that follows the period of greatest development of each. With this method and taking as a basis the supposed experience of anterior cultures, he discovers in the culture of the West the premonitory signs of death. He does not confine himself to that. After having revealed himself as being an expert in the comprehension of the manifestations peculiar to all cultures—which logically and in accord with his own thesis would be intelligible only to those who belong to them—he sets about establishing norms for his own country.

If one were to try to establish the philosophical filiation of Spengler's thought, one could say perhaps that it is linked with the pessimism of Schopenhauer. Spengler himself declares that he is a descendant of Goethe. *The De-*

cline of the West opens with some lines from
Goethe. In any case his presumed philosophy,
be what it may, gives only an external definition
of culture based on its supposed duration.
Waldo Frank, in his *Rediscovery of America*
offers, on the other hand, a leading thought
that allows for the definition of culture if by
culture is meant the full realization of human
life. That realization is achieved only when
the life of both individuals and nations develops within a meaningful whole. Frank does
not accept the fragmentation of the cultures
as made by Spengler. Europe is to him a
living organic body. Its heart, its mind and
its soul, the fountain of its spirit were Egypt,
Judea, Athens and Rome. The Mediterranean is, according to Frank, the womb of
Europe. Spengler has singled out and con-
trasted the different parts of the Mediterranean: this is to the American writer "as
preposterous as trying to disconnect the organs
of a body." If the separation of cultures as
Spengler treats of them were authentic, Helenes
and Jews would not have been able to write in
Alexandria. In Spinoza's *Ethics* Frank
finds the model of what constitutes a culture:
the conscious and creative life of man in a felt
and thought whole. Spinoza is, in fact, the
philosopher that Frank cites with most fre-
quency and admiration. He seems to be his

11

teacher.   At times he appears to be under the
influence of romantic German philosophy and
its North American adherents.   The description
that Frank gives us of man's image and of his
own individual life reminds us at times of
Bergson as does his conception of life as a
perpetual creative process.   His intensely artistic temperament also draws him closer to
the French philosopher.   Bergson's philosophy
is spontaneously the philosophy of an artist.

In Harold Hoffding's *Philosophy of Religion*
are found some ideas that coincide with those
of Frank, as, for example, the agreement of
both in respect to the internal discord that
Protestantism produced in the spirits of men
during modern times.   But in spite of the
possible influences that Frank might have
received in the formation of his mentality, the
fact remains that that mentality is most
individual.   Spengler is not an author that
finds favor in Frank's eyes.   The latter shows,
without directly pointing it out, that Spengler's
invocation of Goethe is not justifiable.   Here
we might quote the American thinker: "The
tradition of conscious Europeanism can be
said to date from Goethe.   Goethe was nourished on Spinoza.   His vision of Europe was
that of a microcosmic whole enhanced by a
profound pantheism; it was at once rational
and naturalistic.   But the world that sur-

rounded this man was breaking up. The dualism of his age was working against his proposition. Goethe himself was a succession of parts that followed each other in a series: the poet of love, the poet of nature, the poet of Faust, the scientist and the man who dreamed of a synthetic Europe. He poured out his mystic essence in his poetry; his organically formed compositions were carefully distributed between his biology and his politics. Hegel, who started out so well, confused the State and the Church of Prussia with the Spinozistic substance. Marx based his whole on the spiritless logic of economics. Nietzsche unified Europe by making it the mold of individual power. Goethe was a great disciple of Spinoza. There has been no great disciple of Goethe."

In opposition to Spengler's disjunction of humanity in time and space, Frank offers the implied thought of the unity of the species. While Spengler is a boastful patriot, Frank is a severe critic of the country he loves. The United States constitutes to his mind a jungle of machines. The American man dragged along by his thirst for wealth is the slave of the machines he has constructed although he is under the illusion that he is their master. The gods and the cults of America are the gods and cults of wealth. The life of the American man drags itself along unconsciously between the

impulsion of power and the luxurious enjoyment of a comfort that is not what it seems to
be. The tumultuous and stupid life of the
American is mechanical. Its tragic misery
born of European disorder will find surcease
only when human existence acquires a human
sense of the whole. While Spengler advocates
a return to the modes of being of the recent
Prussian past, to its essential military col-
lectivism, Frank recommends to his country
the active renovation of the mystical tradition
of America. Facing the evil typified by
American journalism, that "bazaar of news"
which piques the curiosity of the male with the
childish novelty of a toy, stands the American
woman. She was man's good companion.
She followed him when he crossed the continent, she helped him break rocks and open
paths in the wilderness. When America followed in the footsteps of a decomposed Europe,
the woman of necessity had to follow the path
of man's will. In the mechanical process of
Americanization realized so far the North
American woman was delivered to the ruinous
homage of her man. That anomalous era of
the defeminization of the American woman is
drawing to a close. She learned a hard lesson
and the results of that lesson significantly
manifest themselves today in the American
girl. The American woman, according to

Frank, is returning to the fountains of femininity, to a new, discerning femininity which is entirely free of sentimentality. She is regaining woman's legitimate position in the world; within her lies the seed of a new nation.

Confronted with this budding woman of America, the American man must of necessity undergo a change. He will have to raise himself to her level; no longer will he be able to conquer her by plucking the old cords of sentiment, of tradition or of the law, those cords which he himself, as Frank tells us, has cut. And as the American author says: "Perhaps the first step towards the creation of a whole from this American chaos of ours, may be the union of the man with this Eve that was not formed from his rib. . . ."

To Spengler's domestic glorification of Prussianism, Waldo Frank opposes the patriotic American truth. America has been and still is a wild and turbulent chaos. Up to the present time, the intermittent splendours radiated by its mysticism have been too few and far between to assure the creation of eternal fire. Caught between two fires—that of the mistakes she has committed and that of the evils that exist within her, America is at war with herself.

In his *Decline of the West* Spengler offers us a schematic outline of the different cultures that the world has known. In the present

stage of our culture, the culture of the West, he
discovers the unmistakable symptoms of im-
minent collapse.   But he does not stop at that
point, hence his book includes a diagnosis as
well as a prognosis.   Spengler resigns himself
to the fatality of the latter.   Waldo Frank,
on the other hand, with more modesty and
reserve indicates in his *Rediscovery of America*
the characteristics that best define the true
nature of his country.   Its deficiencies and the
signs of its mutilation are forcibly revealed by
the author.   Various ideas peculiar to the
Mediterranean littoral and to European countries that left the work of their civilizations on
that territory assumed fanatical proportions
when they were suddenly transmitted to
America, because they had been torn away
from the primitive whole organisms in which
they were born.

The chaotic state which takes on violent
attributes in the American jungle is in truth
peculiar to the entire modern world.   The
Catholic republic of the Middle Ages was the
last form of coherent culture in Europe.

The chaos from which a new world shall rise
is the result of an imaginative, destructive
process which followed the breaking up of the
structure that represented the classic conception of the whole.   The existence of that chaos
is also due in part to the fact "that each

fragment of that shattered whole survived of its own accord, drawing strength from the belief that it constituted a whole." Thus we see that Frank assigns a most important place in the history of man to the mental factors which represent the spirit. Consequently his doctrine assumes a position radically opposed to that which offers a materialistic conception of history. Waldo Frank also objects to Spengler's fatalistic theory which condemns cultures to the inexorable process that ends in their death. It is within the power of man to grasp the full consciousness of the deficiencies of his life; within his reach is the effort, which if exercised will lead to the comprehension of the coherence of the whole in which man himself will be the pivot of all achievement. Spengler bases his conception of history upon biological formulae. Cultures are born, they grow, and they gradually decline until they become extinct. Waldo Frank, on the other hand, conceives of life as a process of continuous creation in which mind prefigures the images created. A human being can enjoy the full benefits of complete living only if his life corresponds to a meaningful whole. Aristotle and Saint Thomas among others are examples of classic wholes. It is now America's turn to create an analogous ideal of complete unity which shall bear the individual stamp of her

personality.   Waldo Frank does not advocate
the return to any culture of the past; "there
is no golden age in all history worthy of being
regained."   The examples of the past are to
be esteemed only in such measure as they can
serve to inspire us through comparison.

The abstract biological formulae which constitute the framework of Spengler's doctrine
do not appeal to the American author: "The
universal will to live is to him a romantic
falsehood; the eternal instincts of self-preserva-
tion and survival are but myths."   Each one
should shape his life in relation to the human
element in man and in regard to the unifying
creations of art.   Frank offers his country and
all America the alternative of a rebirth led
along a new path that stresses the mystic
tradition, or death.   The possibility of death
could become a reality in spite of our powerful
instinct of selfpreservation.

While Spengler resigns himself to the in-
exorability of destiny, Waldo Frank pierces
the veil that hides the future of his America,
of the America whose present shortcomings he
so cruelly exposes.   Waldo Frank thinks of
Spengler as the author of a poem in which the
metaphysical and esthetic notions of the day
are the characters and the subject-matter.
He points out the abstract character of his
"cultures."   Spengler defends his own concep-

tion of death.   His readers' enthusiasm for this
poem is accounted for by the fact that most of
them prefer the certainty of death to the
challenge of a further spiritual development.
Frank does not fear this challenge, he seeks it.
And in his own fashion, with great enthusiasm
and faith in the future of his country and his
continent he marks the boundaries of the
future. Like the prophets, after punishing he
consoles. His is not a consolation of peaceful
contemplation but one of exhortation to the
conscious, spiritual task in which both the
individual and the masses must do their share.
Those who should shoulder the greatest moral
responsibility are the groups of the chosen few
who succeed in perceiving and fully understanding the present shortcomings of man and
his future needs.

The last part of Frank's book is constructive
rather than critical. It is the work of an
educator who feels keenly the responsibility
of what he says and advises. In him there is
something of the prophet and the missionary.
This should not surprise us. John Dewey, the
most widely-read thinker of his country at the
present time, excels equally in philosophy and
in the science of education. The interest that
Americans are showing for pedagogical problems in the broadest sense of the word, is clear
proof of the fact that America's outstanding

minds are not satisfied with the present state of things.

Waldo Frank's message to his countrymen best reveals the wide discrepancy that exists between the American and the German thinker. Spengler's native land is, to his mind, a proud fragment of Europe; her ideas are the best. There is nothing others can teach her. No example set up for her benefit would be of use to her. In order to realize all that life has to offer her, she need but return to the Prussian forms which prevailed before the war. He considers England the cursed country because, together with the Jews, she has discovered the ideas and the methods which have corroded Germany's pristine mode of being. But if Germany is to be an isolated body within Europe, although Spengler does not always openly confess it, she will have to reject the solidarity of the despised nations. That will occur when all of Europe has to confront the Bolshevik peril. Russia will eventually be excluded from the concert of the civilization whose death struggle Spengler sings to martial Prussian music. *Socialism and Prussianism* reveals the theme that lies back of Spengler's whole doctrine: the nationalistic and retrograde chauvinism. His cry is the plaintive wail of a defeated soldier in the midst of an orchestration in which the ghosts of the dead cultures artificially pass in review.

What is Frank's attitude toward the human world? What procedure is America to follow in her relations with other countries and continents? Frank discusses this question in the XIXth chapter of *The Rediscovery of America*. Russia, Europe and the South American countries are three immense human realities in respect to which our budding America will have to define her position. The groups of leaders who will undertake their task bearing in mind the image of America as a human example, as both an American and a universal paradigm, will have to follow a very different procedure from that advocated by Spengler. The problem of soviet Russia will interest the American who foresees the future because there a crucial experiment is now being carried on. "It is nothing less than an attempt to raise the basis of human life above the level of the nutritive." It is an attempt to disanimalize man. This very day the American 'who boasts of devoting all his time to business puts himself on a level with the cow that spends all her time grazing.' The human masses live for the purpose of eating. Neither the United States, France, nor England has made any attempt to put an end to this abject state of affairs. The countries of the West, like Greece and Rome, are empires of slave. In America the economic problem is not to be solved by Russian meth-

ods. The ways and means of the American
jungle and the Russian steppes will not be
identical. But for the American group, whose
appearance Waldo Frank desires and foresees,
this single fact will be an incentive to action:
in Russia an economic and mystical attempt
is being made to give human dignity to the
life of man.

Both of the Americas have risen from the
death throes of the Christian republic, as has
modern Europe itself. Europe together with
America has been undergoing a process of
Americanization which in the Old World has
given rise to special forms of Americanization.
The vestiges of extinct Christianity tend to
hold in check the process which in the New
World is at the height of its development.
Yet Europe is striving in its own way to restore
the lacking whole. The most recent results
of its efforts fade into insignificance when compared with the achievement of the long-
vanished medieval state.

America should understand Europe. She
should try to keep in harmony with her.
The United States will have to change her
method of procedure with the South American
countries if she wishes to prevent them from
assuming the hostile attitude towards her which
Europe maintains. The group of farsighted
Americans will strive to resist Americanization;

the mystical, not the utilitarian tradition
should succeed the mechanical and sterile cult
of wealth. Thus she will form, not a blind
mass dangerous to the world, but a symphonic
nation. Then she will count upon the solidarity of Hispano-America. In the process of the
creation of the continent "there will be two
persons," says Frank, "of whom we may perhaps
be the male, she the female." In the creation
of harmony between the two continents, the
United States must take the initiative. Europe
will probably prove to be a creator and a re-
ceptor. Her great men will turn towards the
new world; not to assume an attitude of self-
defense but to regard it with an open mind.
This is entirely feasible. America, situated
between the two poles, and again between
three continents, is fabulously rich in spirit and
strength. "If wealth does not reduce her to
ashes, she will be a sun that illuminates the
world of men." Sympathy towards the Soviet
experiment, brotherhood on the continent,
and confidence in Europe are the three man-
dates that Frank proclaims to the best minds
of his country.

Sintesis, Buenos Aires

15

Waldo Frank, Thinker and Poet

BY

P. González Casanova

I should have liked to entitle this article, "Waldo Frank, Philosopher," if a fortuitous circumstance had not dissuaded me. On a recent occasion, when he heard himself referred to as a philosopher, Frank turned up his nose at the name. "I am not a philosopher: I am simply a writer." "A thinker," amended Oliverio Toro, courteously and deferentially. "And a poet," anyone who has read his *Virgin Spain* would add.

In reality, poet and thinker, novelist and philosopher, Frank is all in one. The last name may weigh upon his natural modesty or upon the moral repugnance which a title so badly outworn and abused can inspire in him. Nevertheless, I shall avoid giving it to him in order not to clash with his way of feeling; but I shall not leave off speaking of his philosophy. There is no need for this. The name of Hesiod is not accompanied by this title either, and although, perhaps because of it, he is not ranked with Aristotle and Plato in the history of philosophy, his considerable influence in ethical and religious thought does not admit of any doubt. It is also true that the cosmological speculation of the Ionian school began only a century and a half after his epoch; Hesiod, therefore, preceded the dawn of Hellenic philosophy. And in this respect he does not coincide with Frank who appears at the hour of the decline of western philosophy. But is there no resemblance between dawn and dusk?

In a prescientific era, like that of Hesiod, or in an ultrascientific one like our contemporaneous world, it is logical to expect the poet to penetrate nature and life, flinging far from him worn-out formulae, however old their stamp, many already valueless; and, taking as his only guide his intuition, to try to arrive at the ethical and aesthetic solutions that concern him so profoundly and directly.

But Frank should not be compared because of this with Spengler, as is usually done. He has little or nothing in common with the author of *The Decline of the West* unless it be what the latter has of the poet in his brilliant apocalyptical exposition.

Does not Spengler invite us, after predicting an era of material greatness, but only material, to prepare for adapting ourselves to the new structure, and this at the time when that material greatness threatens to smother the

ethical and aesthetic flame of occidental culture
and to destroy it?

Furthermore: Spengler would like us to aban-
don all hope of saving ourselves from disaster
with our rancid ideals which he accuses of being
nebulous and formless. Such an effort would
be fruitless, according to him, and we should—
submissive to destiny—apply ourselves immediately to the scientific organization of the
new age which begins for the world in the
present. *"Ducunt fata volentem, nolentem
trahunt,"* say, fatidically, the words that close
his work.

Before that haunting vision of our materialistic age, the tragic attitude of Spengler—
prophet of misfortunes, contemplating the
disappearance of his world of the past—
contrasts with the heroic, Promethean-like
attitude of Frank, poet, man of the future who,
in the world that is being born and that is his,
wishes to revive the flame of the redeeming fire
—the menaced flame that is the right of the
spirit. And that same fire shines in his glance,
kindles it—without perturbing his habitual
kindness and gentleness—giving to his clear,
seer-like eyes, the profound and serene expression of the eyes of children who begin to live;
scrutinizing eyes of eternity, which are open,
inquiring about the past and the future.

And then the thinker and poet speak in
Frank.

The first, the thinker, examines severely
yet with serenity the present evils, their
causes, their sources in the past; but from the
depths of this past it is the poet who draws
forth whatever of nobility and beauty, of light,
and truth they contain, measuring them
against our actual civilization and our coarse
materialistic atmosphere; and it is the prophet
in him, the seer, who penetrates the shadowed
centuries before us, and extracts promise
from the darkness we are entering and which
will last for centuries.   He is like the diver who
reappears from the bottom of a sea of mud and
mire to the surface with hands full of precious
stones: faith, virtues, all the noble ambitions
of the man of yesterday, of the man of tomorrow, of the man of all time when he is
worthy of being called a man.

This is why Frank is and must continue to be
a guide for youth.   He inspires youth—the
young in years and in soul—to seek with him
the word of redemption for the spirit, that
today is almost strangled in the claws of the
black beast—contemporary materialistic civilization.

It is Frank's idea that weapons of spiritual
defense, against moral sensualism, against
aggressive capitalism—against all the spawn
of an unbalanced culture—can be found, solid,
multiform, and efficient, in the heart of the

12

Hispano-American people. He loves Spain and professes to find in its spiritual heirs the virtues which he admires so much in the mother nation. And still more: before the menace of common danger, North American imperialism invites them to unite. For union is possible only if Yankee imperialism consents first to extend the routes of communication from Rio Grande to the Straits of Magellan, thus establishing a bond of union to those peoples, today so distant.

Frank never remains in the realm of the unattainable. The idea must be followed by action. The danger having been noticed, and the inner force acknowledged that may be opposed to it with hopes of success, it must produce a method, a discipline of the spirit that fortifies the soul, that feeds man and gives him strength to attack and conquer the new Medusa.

From chaos, order; from confusion, harmony; such is the inspiration of the aesthetician— since he does not wish to be called philosopher.

And Frank, the poet, inspired by the thoughts that he has unsealed from the Upani-shad, the Pentateuch, the Gospel, Ancient and Modern Philosophy, knows how to carry on his enterprise. Not as an apostle, but as a guide.

He shows us the path that we have left

behind, over which we have travelled in
various millennia, and which comes to end
today in the abyss of materialism, chaos, and
confusion.   But it is not possible to stop, to
return, to undo what has been done.   We
must go on, yes, but also we must be vigilant
so that the flame of the spirit that awaits
us is not extinguished in the secular night
ahead.   The voice of the poet and thinker is
alert; inspired, it radiates emotion, and hope.
It is not the voice of the orator of decadence,
of the juggler with sonorous and hollow words.
Waldo Frank's is the serene voice of the man
of faith, of faith capable of moving mountains;
it is the voice of a man whose truth is the
truth.

El Universal, Mexico

16

WALDO FRANK, CRITIC AND DESTROYER

BY

FRANCISCO DURO

A Far-seeing Prophet

Some forty years ago, a certain English writer, Sir William Hurrell Mallock, a Protestant, at any rate he certainly wasn't a Catholic, published in London, in successive issues of *The Nineteenth Century and After*, an interesting essay which he entitled, *Is Life Worth Living?* Reverend Forbes, a Jesuit father, changed this title in his French translation to *La vie, vaut-elle la peine de vivre?*

I haven't that book, which in my youthful days seemed quite remarkable; but the present reading of Waldo Frank's books and of his lectures has very strongly reminded me of it. And not entirely without motive, as my reader will see.

Alarmed by the invasion of Spencerian doctrines, which at that time were exploding in the university lecture-hall, in books, in literary and scientific reviews, in the daily papers and in novels which most directly reach and influence the masses, this British

essayist began to question if after all, once the
ends of existence had been united to the present
life, and all notion of a life after death and all
hope of justice beyond the grave had been
blotted from the mind of future man, and there
had been imposed upon every stage of human
activity in particular, and upon the whole of
the masses, the postulates of the struggle for
existence, of the prepotency of the strongest
who at the same time probably constitute the
selection of the fittest—if there would not
be fatally aroused within each man the beast
which he carries within him, dragging society,
in the midst of groups having a certain superficial air of civilization, back to a really savage
state.

The Realization of the Prophecy

Now, half a century later, we find a North
American, relentlessly and smilingly making a
vivisection of society in books and in lectures
(which attract large audiences) for the sole
purpose of answering *ex post facto* the question
of that British essayist. Face to face with
that region of the world which boasts of a
high degree of general well-being and of the
more solid values of human civilization, i.e.,
with his native country, North America,
Frank recognizes that "amoral Positivism"
is consummating the complete destruction of the

Christian synthesis, reducing to an outlandish excess the disintegration begun at the time of the Protestant Reformation; and recognizes also that the sociological aphorism of Hobbes, "*homo homini lupus,*" has real value and a practical effect upon each of us, living within the present social circle. He sees that the triumphal egoism which he calls "Power" prevents all human hierarchy so that there is no authority of one over the rest; and that it permits no form of society which is not herd-like when peaceful; and, when turbulent, a bellowing and clawing in a jungle. He recognizes that there can be no real capacity for home-building and family-life among human beings of equal egotistical tendencies and antagonistic to each other, when the men like machines and the women like mannish creatures seek only to satisfy their selfish selves. It is his belief that Europe is floundering in chaos just as much as America; perhaps America is in greater danger than Europe. To sum it up, if the present life of man is foul to those who are enjoying it in their vulgar fashion, then it turns out to be rather loathsome and full of anguish for those of us who still keep, in the depth of our souls, some remnant of spiritual desire. He confesses also to having noticed indecency and sadness in Buenos Aires, in spite of his short stay in the capital city of Argentina.

Chaos, Agony and Death

Frank has written all this in his books and he gives it directly to his many audiences, although, since his communication is oral and he is present, it is necessary to veil some concepts and to soften crude expressions which might be considered disrespectful. The lectures, therefore, repeat the books; and though both books and lectures are already quite numerous, the group of ideas is always the same, and the forms of expression in the written part just as in the spoken occur in a successive hammering, which becomes monotonous, dulls the attention, and results in fatiguing the reader as well as the listener. The worst is that on closing the book, the same as on rising from one's chair, while admiring the over-abundant mental and literary exertion of the writer or lecturer, and while almost agreeing with his profound criticism of the present, one cannot help noticing the utter lack of any standards of orientation for efficient action in the future; and one senses a certain feeling of pessimism in the very depths of his soul, which still retains a yearning for all those noble things which are now covered by that pompous and empty term "spiritual values." To put it briefly, Frank writes and comes to tell us the same thing the historian Titus Livy told the decadent subjects of the first Roman

CAESARS: *nec mala, nec remedia pati possunt.*
You can no longer suffer either your evils or
the medicine to cure them.

My reader will find an obvious reminiscence
of this concept in a paragraph delivered, the
21st of October in the Hall of Lectures, before
a very large audience. "I have been here
sufficiently long," said Frank, "to note that
the mortal chaos of the old worlds exists in
this country, too. Perhaps in your provinces
(as in ours) fragments of old human thoughts
still persist. But here in Buenos Aires, which
is the head and conscious crystal of your nation,
the modern chaos is excessively advanced.
Buenos Aires is no longer a part of Europe.
Nor will it ever be. That part of it which is
imitating Paris (as we used to imitate London)
is stuttering lifeless words, without taste or
meaning. Paris itself, I assure you, is dying.
It is living its autumn days. But what in
Buenos Aires is Europe is not dying at all;
it hasn't even life enough to die."

The Critic

I find, therefore, in the work of this North
American writer two parts of unequal value:
criticism and that which pretends to be constructive. In the first, Frank sees clearly and
conveys intimately to his reader or listener
all the anti-social egoism and anarchism of our

present life. From this triumphal egoism which he calls "Power," there has arisen dynamism, and from this the machine. The machine which is the creation of modern man is, at the same time, his principal oppressor. The machine invented in order to produce, that is to say, in order to sell, products for the purpose of accumulating wealth, is not a providential aid to anyone, not even to its owner, who lives in perpetual anxiety trying to supply the demands of his machine, and in a state of constant watchfulness, in order to equal or excel the machine of his competitor, in his own country or in some other foreign country.

The great daily newspaper, made up especially of news and (within the classification of news) of the most spectacular and resounding crimes, constitutes another factor of "Power" and of demoralization. News is, for the common public, *what games are* to the wilful and badly educated child. The newspaper, observes Frank, is our predominant popular art. . . . The rôle which the people plays in this art is passive, because our people, too, are passive. News is a toy—the plaything of a child whose hankering has been cunningly stimulated and whose hands hold a handful of coins. The toys of the child are useless things, artificially and exclusively concocted to be playthings. But the news of the press,—

is it perhaps the serious events of the whole
world? The daily news of our newspapers
bears the same relation to reality as the toy
cat or motor bears to the real cat or motor.
. . . Accuracy is not demanded of the newspaper but rather novelty. Not reality but
graphic presentation is requested. Not originality, but instead of that a cheap emotional appeal, in such a way that the reader
can identify the story without any effort, with
his own inclination illusions. Remember that
definition: "A dog bites a man; that is no
news. But a man bites a dog; that *is* news."
The prints are full of adulteries and crimes;
and yet it will be observed not everybody
commits them. Certainly not: Everyone does
not commit them, but everyone wants them.
So-called good "news" is the symbol of what
everybody needs but cannot have; like a "good
toy,"—symbol of what every child needs but
cannot have, except in that symbol. . . . Until
the public becomes "mature," the reading of
news will be for it just a plaything; and there
will never be anything to which it will give
more importance than to these playthings.
The real problem is not to give the common
herd a nourishment superior to its understanding, and therefore beyond its needs.

The American gods of Power, Frank also
tells us, have a temple. That is the expression

of the best we can offer of our worth, and of
our love; we have given it the name of skyscraper. Fifty stories, one on top of another,
express a herd. . . . We are a mass rigidly
compressed within a simple structure. Our
rank is equalitarianism; our aim is height; action
our dynamic; our most definite value, the
Power of the majority. So that the structure
which represents us has for its goal immensity,
and for its system, the monotonous piling up
of sameness upon sameness.

In like manner, all factors of the social
evolution of his country file past the keen
eyes of the North American essayist; the
worship of success, literature, associations or
corporations, politics, sports, sex, legislation,
official charity and philanthropy, remnants of
the old religious Puritanism, spiritualism,
theosophy; and in general, any dispassionate
reader or listener might go on agreeing with
his criticisms, grateful for the leading thread
which guides him through complex matters
which heretofore his own field of vision, has
recognized but vaguely.

Yet if knowledge of the evils is not to put in
our possession the remedies to cure them, what
good can it bring? Frank fears such a possible
reproach, predicting for both North and South
America an internal vitality capable of re-
constructing the disjointed social system and of

regenerating man both individually and so-
cially. Argentina has not yet been born. It
is a potential nation still in a state of pregnancy.
It still has no God; it is reaching the stage of
birth through an increasing development. We
must go downwards into the soil, right within
us. In this dimension of profundity, the
Argentinians will discover their God, a discovery which they need in order to become a
nation.

Words, words, words. Beyond which, however, one finds this assertion explicitly and
fundamentally certain: "The problem of the
modern world is not basically economic, it is a
religious problem, a human problem. The
world is comprised of men. If the world is to
change, then man must change." How? By
what means? With whose help? Following
what norms of action? I shall explain, according to Frank, in another article.

The Catholic thinkers, fighting against individualistic liberalism and its socialistic and
communistic derivations, preceded Hurrell
Mallock by many years, in foreseeing and
announcing the nearness of the chaos which
now appears to Frank as a state definitely
reached. The day following the Revolution
of 1848, which dethroned Louis Philippe in
Paris, Proudhon hurled into the face of the
world these terrible assertions: "Ownership is

robbery"; "God is evil"; "Whoever tries to
govern me is a tyrant and a usurper; I declare
him my enemy." There stood out among the
defenders of God, of ownership and of Christian
order, against the aphorisms of that violent
anarchist, an insuperable book by the Spaniard,
Donoso Cortés, whom Frank undoubtedly does
not know. It is really a pity that he does not
know him. Donoso Cortés did not lack dissenters in the Catholic fold. According to
Frank himself, there are always those who are
afraid that the Gospel be too truthful. The
bishop of Orleans, Monsignor Dupanloup, who
had contacts with political liberalism, had his
cassock publicly torn off by a representative
who exclaimed: "This man blasphemes."

It is certain nonetheless that the author of
the "Essay on Catholicism, Liberalism and Socialism" proved himself inexorable. His logic
was obstreperous, and his deductions completely pessimistic. He recognized in socialism
and in communism the simple products of
liberal doctrinarianism. The denial by states
of God and His ordinance ends in a denial of
the states themselves. When governments
separate from God, they instinctively feel the
lack of power to punish. First the crimes
committed against social order stop being
punished, then later even the crimes against
individuals. He who yesterday was a criminal,

today is called eccentric or insane. The
modern rationalizers call crime a "misfortune."
The day will come when the government will
pass into the hands of such "unfortunates"
and then there will be no crime punishable,
other than that of innocence. The new gospel
of the world is probably being written in some
penitentiary. The world will get nothing but
what it deserves when the world becomes
evangelized by the new apostles. The same
ones who have made people believe that the
earth could be a Paradise, have made them
believe even more easily that the world is to
be a. Paradise without blood. Evil does not
lie in illusion; it lies in the fact that at the
moment when illusion is believed by all, then
blood bursts forth, even from the very rocks,
and the Earth will be transformed into Inferno.
On this obscure and lonely earth, man cannot
aspire to an impossible happiness without being
so wretched as not to lose that little happiness
he has salvaged for himself.

When the readers, in the presence of all this,
exclaimed: "*Durus est hic sermo*," Donoso
Cortés answered: "I confess my book has come
to light at the wrong time; it has appeared
before when it should have appeared *after*
the deluge. In the flood all will be drowned
but I, that is to say, everyone's doctrines but
mine. Then what a disaster there will be;

one will see how the wrecked ones seek refuge
in my port, although even that may not happen
since some will prefer the salty seas to any
haven at all. Each one to his own taste. . . ."

The era announced by Donoso Cortés from
the Catholic field in 1850, and thirty years
later by Sir Hurrell Mallock from the camp of
English Protestantism, is what Frank is presenting now, from the field of agnosticism in
North America; it is what he calls a return to
barbarism.

Donoso Cortés foresaw, floating in the wreck,
the sublime figure of Christ, eternally repeat-
ing: "I am the way, the truth, the light."
The English writer said, in opposition, that
since Christ had been repulsed, he did not see
whence in the future would come the word of
life. Mr. Frank, buffeted back and forth by
the waves, tells us that salvation will come
from ourselves.

This assertion strikes me as being stupendous.
I shall try to appreciate it in another article
from the Catholic's point of view. While this
process of social decomposition continues, our
attitude should be, according to the recommendation of Frank, to accept the machine
which imposes itself upon us, and to accept the
increase in the general comforts of material
life which it is gaining for us, preparing ourselves to replace them with a "positive"

creation.   We have the crude material in our "magnificent chaos."   Now that "a new spirit and new energy are needed to hammer into shape from the materials of this chaos, a new system into which it is destined to change," Waldo Frank, who is a Spinozistic Pantheist, offers them to us with pleasure.   Therefore, I shall examine the golden apple of Yankee origin, so cheerfully offered to us. . . .

Criterio, Buenos Aires

17

Waldo Frank

Since the publication in book form of our *Ideario Nuclear*, this is the first time that DIOGENES appears. We thought it effective to leave the seed, hidden underground, to its intricate process of germination. As was logical and necessary, the first reaction of our environment was silence and rebuff. Our ideology was answered with silence—extreme weapon, to which strength and weakness alike revert; and the wrathful diatribe, humorously disproportionate, responded to our restrictive judgments on the presumptions of value of the intellectuals. We did not expect greater success than that obtained. Upon negative impulse, inspired by the blind desire for power, there will gradually appear positive gratitude from the ruins of the intellectual faction which we have helped to demolish. There will gradually rise the new state of spiritual consciousness for which we strive. Not by our work, of course, but thanks to the action of two coinciding forces: command of the times which comes from the outside and the evolutionary wave that comes from the depth of our *argentinidad*. The anxiety to "get ahead" derived from frantic individualism, which characterizes the intellectuals today, will be substituted in the future by an idealistic desire, fruit of the collective opinion, as an expression of the common soul.

We could not invoke a more propitious name for the new departure of the cynic of Synope— who not without a certain unwillingness leaves the cell of his tub—than that of Waldo Frank. This austere leader of the forces that Diogenes propounds and praises comes to us—Latin-America—with protecting arms from the country of "The Jungle." His is the first cordial voice of brotherly accents which that factory of the world utters. It indicates that the unbridled force is being humanized. Supposing that a luminous spot appears in that obscure conscience, there still remains a redeeming hope for the giant of iron muscles who has transfused his pure immortal essence into arms and legs. The sharp, fearless criticisms aimed by Frank against the indifferent rostrum of his people resound in the heart of future America, which we all bear within, in gestation, as the crowing of the cock announcing the dawn. The acrimony that Frank expresses in his negation of power is encouraging because it denotes the volume of his capacity for love. It has already been said that all future heaven is born from an equivalent inferno in the soul of him who conceives it.

It is certain for us that the age of nuclearism has begun. The romantic movement of the spirit which leads to analytic disintegration, being exhausted, the ascending parabola of the creating integration arises. An example of this is Keyserling, the first attempt at intellectual totalization of diverse cultures. And another no less expressive is Waldo Frank in his intrepid effort to integrate America. With fine spiritual penetration he has begun the study of Latin-America by way of Spain. And that study reveals to us—the arc of the parabola being insinuated in it—that the discovery and conquest of this continent are incidents of such magnitude that they have not even been arranged by human thought. Perhaps in order to wholly comprehend the present it may first be necessary to have complete knowledge of the cultural elements and the latent values which will determine the incorporation of America in the civilized world.

One of the most pointed things which have been said of Spain is that which Frank sets forth in *España Virgen:* "The Spaniard has not been able to rule Spain because he has always given too much thought to establishing the kingdom of God on earth and to counterbalancing his contradictory impulses." Such is, in effect, Spanish destiny, which our peoples have inherited from their lineage: to establish

the kingdom of God on earth, and in man
harmony between impulses and the spirit.
Therefore, the ethical sense is the dominating
note of all Spanish life. Frank, however, has
omitted this fundamental phase, preoccupied,
as it were, with tracing large architectural lines.
He has not, for that very reason, taken into
account the spiritual work of Ganivet—*Traba-
jos de Pío Cid* and *Conquista del Reino de Maya*
—which is of greater meaning with regard to
the evolutionary life of the Iberian character.

And so it is that Frank, more than a psy-
chologist, is a great constructor. There is in
him, perhaps, the rising impulse of the skyscrapers, of the gigantic magnitudes, polarized
by the sense of elegance and the taste of the
inlaid work of Arabian architecture. The
landscape, before his eyes, rises in solids, planes,
and lines which disappear in the remoteness
of their origin. This quality has made it
possible for him to trace the arc of the circle
which goes from sunny Iberia to New York.
It likewise impels him to extend the straight
lines which permit America to appear with a
unity of character that it now lacks. A great
architectural artist is Waldo Frank and in that
rôle we can acknowledge him the first Herald
of America. But, perhaps, his constructive
power has made him forget the cultivation of
the vital element. There is much steel and

cement in his sumptuous structures despite
what is subtilized in elegant volutes. That
perhaps is why they resemble the severe skyscrapers, which disappear into space like Gothic
cathedrals; but while these symbolize, as
"stone memorials," the Christian spirit which
rises toward eternity, the skyscrapers raise
their bulk, cathedrals of power, as a defiance to
spiritual values.

Although the expression may savor of para-
dox, it could be said of Frank that he prophesies
the past. His vision of Spain—baroque
architecture—as his pathetic picture of America—modern architecture, of smooth planes
which oscillate between the factory and the
prison—constitute inert images, seen with
intemporal eyes from the bowels of yesterday.
It may be, in effect, the past aspiring to repeat
itself, to persist in enduring, and that is the
generating attitude of decomposition and catas-
trophe. In the presence of that blind rotating
shuttle which has lost the regulating bridle,
Waldo Frank's conscience awakens and announces the fall of Babylon with biblical
intonations. And the prophesy is true, un-
assailable. But perhaps Frank may not have
noticed that he formulates his present ana-
themas in the name of the past to which it is
impossible for us to return. As if to say that
the luxury of Plato tramples upon another

kind of luxury.   What are the forces or values
that Frank invokes to condemn the kingdom of
Power?   He opposes only the principle of love.
But it is now nineteen centuries since the law
of love was proclaimed from the cross; and
one of its results is the civilization which
Frank repudiates so vehemently.   The will
to power which is, in short, the objective
expression of instinct has elaborated its technique; and he can meet it only with the
technique of ethics and of the spirit.   Waldo
Frank suspects something of this and therefore
he proposes, at the end of his *Rediscovery*, a
mental exercise of the Loyola kind, as a weapon
for combating the organization of power.
We greatly fear that that instrument will
change into one more expedient for guarantee-
ing individualistic control.

For it is a fact that Waldo Frank does not
renounce intellectualism.   It is probable that
he is comfortably settled in the ethos brought
about by those men who are bringing it to our
country and forcing it on us.   And the substantial disposition of these men is a devotion
to power much more fervent than that of any
Yankee of fanatic patriotism.   The only per-
ceptible difference is that the desire for power,
in them, is of an intellectual character.   But a
kingdom of intellectualistic power would be
much more sad and implacable than the wilful

power of the United States. To combat that power and to aspire to the consolidated command of ethic values, Diogenes is a leper among the intellectual caste that fondles and entertains our guest.

Frank speaks of the United States as a country that has hypertrophied subordinate values and has forgotten to incorporate the supreme values already created. And that in our judgment is not the case. It would be, rather, that of a people that has continued the development of the lineage of Europe and has come to the point where European values, evolved to the extreme of hypertrophy, threaten chaos and must be superseded. Frank's error consists in implicitly supposing that said superior values exist or are improvised by meditative exercises. It is now more than a century that Argentina, resting upon the Iberian heritage, has been trying to fashion such values, by imprinting them in her subconscious character. The lineage of that life, which Almafuerte symbolized with his integral ethicism, acts in diverse fields with purified reforming energy and sustains ruthless battle against the intellectual power which it represents to the European world. There is evident proof that the supercession of the values of North America will be no easy task.

Frank has seen justly in proposing the creation of groups; which would be equivalent

to transferring to the spiritual plane the
collective sense realized in the plane of the
will by the North American community.
Such is, in reality, the only solution which
might supersede the reign of power. But the
creation of a substance which surpasses power
is previously required—and this Frank does
not seem to suspect: an essential substance
founded on the vital nucleus of life which finds
its own finality in itself and may be capable of
using as instruments all the other values.
This is what the *gaucho* has realized among us
because, as S. Anderson said, culture always
grows in the hands of the laborers. And then,
it is still necessary to find the technical formula
of spiritual evolution, and of an adaptation to
reality that permits the intellectuals, gifted
with sufficient wisdom and idealism, to identify
themselves fundamentally without mutilating
or oppressing their characteristic individuality.
That is the laborious task to which the Nucleo
Diogenes is pleased to commit itself, and in
which it hopes to count upon the sympathy of
the North American Zarathustra.

All things considered from a superior plane,
North America deserves the gratitude of
humanity. It has closed, with its action, the
evolutionary circle of instrumental power,
necessary and essential base for ascent to a
higher plane. Now that horizon is sealed.

He who does not feel desirous of embarking on new undertakings will have to submit himself to the American's implacable yoke. But he who does not resign himself to the renouncement of his dream—the ambition of creating the kingdom of God on earth—may enter into the Argentinian ranks and collaborate on the epic poem that will clinch the dominion of man over life. In that growing cycle the honor of forerunner belongs to Waldo Frank.

Diógenes, La Plata

18

Meditation on Waldo Frank

BY

Juan Marinello

All the work of Waldo Frank is an athletic, unrelenting struggle between vision and idea. Waldo Frank has seen Spain in a new light, because he is at once immersed in and removed from the quixotic conception, namely, will and irony, which so characterizes Spain. As in the hero of Cervantes, as resurrected lately by Frank, reality is a necessary factor for truth but does not preempt it. When Don Quixote suspects that Sancho Panza is in the right, that what he considers a helmet of gold, might well be a barber's shaving dish, he affirms the legendary character of the object, without attempting, by a path beset with doubts, the journey to reality. The heroic, genuine impulse must emerge unchanged in spite of any clash with the tangible world. The real cannot trespass beyond the limits of possibility into the quixotic world. The acceptance of logical and analytical wisdom by the squire during the mock heroics at the Duke's and Duchess's arouses the perturbed anxiety of the Hero.

Everything ought to remain as a contrast, as a background to the heroic will. A world in which justice is ridiculed is needed so that the crusade for justice's sake be efficacious. If the reality which beclouds justice is perceived by the Hero, the crusade comes to an end.

Waldo Frank proceeds like Don Quixote. He knows that the Basques were remarkable navigators, founding colonies in crucial times from Canada to Argentina, thus furthering the will of Spain. This is reality. Truth is the primitive man, the Basque, the epitome of uncivilized and instinctive behavior, impervious to the Roman, to the Mussulman, to Roldan, to the Visigoths, and to the zealous plan of Isabel the Catholic. Truth is the man-island clinging to the mountains of Guipuzcoa. And as reality is a thing apart from but parallel to the real, the Basque will represent in himself, in Argentina, in Canada—the impenetrability of his mountains.

The author of *The Rediscovery of America* found the key for opening the doors of Spain. Now he prepares to penetrate into Iberic America. The key to Spain is not a useful one for arriving at the core of the settlements colonized by her. The City, the central hero in the work of Waldo Frank, is not Spanish; nor is it Spanish in Cuba nor in Bolivia. The colonial has ceased to exist—nor did he in his essence participate in the Castilian will and since he has not even erected any towers, there are none to overthrow. He is a man who did not possess truth and does not as yet possess reality. How can one whose worry over the dispersed whole has not as yet acquired even a partial measuring rod for his realization, how can such a one fruitfully regulate a world?

But, suppose the culmination of the instinctive tendency to establish a new order, a new truth were not fatal? Suppose South America rescues on the shoulders of its incipient and frustated reality that eagerness of the whole of the Spanish atom without the heroic proceedings initiated and completed by each atom? What if, as in Spain, the chaos in the land discovered during her imperial reign were the forerunner and integrator of its unity?

Hitherto Waldo Frank has discussed the past and the present. Spanish America invites, obliges one to scrutinize the future. The philosophic and esthetic content of the books of the great essayist encompasses the City, and the Man who has crystallized its spirit. The future is discerned in each one of his books as a fatal development of its particular forces. Or as a contradiction—also fatal—of its forces. It is that which is congruent with the spectator who, serenely passionate, carries the banners of truth. This is dominant,

superior to reality; and to isolate it, it is necessary to detach it from the background of true
facts, by a process that may render it significant. Thus it is that Waldo Frank is the
historian and the interpreter of wholes, the
understanding artist of the occult curves that
are strengthening at the point at which they
diverge.

The approach to the future is to be through
enthusiasm and political engineering. Hence,
an inhibition to the purely critical qualities.
And the banishment of speculations susceptible only of intellectual substantiation. Waldo
Frank—as it has been so often repeated these
days—is not a writer for any specific nostrum.
His sincere stand as a critic of history—past
and present—prevents him from taking such a
stand. He does not possess the annihilating
irreconcilability of the politically-minded man.
Were he to possess it, he would have at his
disposal the arm of his truth. He would be
the son, not the critic of heroic truth.

Spanish America can be truth, because the
resolution of its chaos lies in the future and
because the people of Spanish America are not
able to live fully in the present or have they the
energy to diverge from it—that is why Spanish
America is for Waldo Frank a political theme.
Will his conceptions preserve their clear
profundity among the deluding shadows of our

world?   Will the frame of his ideas be in agreement with a distant unity?   Because we await it, our devotion deepens for this extraordinary American, who understands the truth in the heart of a people which desires a transcendent category for its gigantic and painful realities.

Revista de Avance, Habana

C. THE ARTIST

19

Waldo Frank: Novelist

BY

Julio Fingerit

1. Waldo Frank was born August 25, 1889, in Long Branch, N. Y. He is of Jewish parentage but does not profess the Mosaic creed; he adheres to a natural religion— pantheism. He has revealed his sympathies with medieval civilisation and Catholic culture. He has published six volumes of novels and short stories, and in addition six volumes of essays. He is a master in the art of the essay and in that of the novel and the short story. He might have been a writer of good short stories and novels, had he not preferred the rank of a widely discussed and questioned experimentalist. He does not wish to devote himself to an art that is already canonised, but rather to his own experiences of art. He prefers to write short stories and novels; but he is not disposed to narrate a story from which the life of the protagonist emerges gradually, naturally, as a result of the inspired faith and

the esthetic veracity of the narrator. Frank believes that in this manner many things still unknown are lost, and many things already known are repeated. It is true that this method is primitive and eternal: it is that of the tales of the Chinese, the Negroes, the Malays, the Hebrews, and the Hindus, that of the Catholic tales of the Middle Ages, the tales of Grimm, and the tales of Tolstoi. The method is old, and here we have an artist who is interested only in the new. But very few who have something novel to offer make their appearance in the world. The tales of men of all time are the story of man; and the story of the man of a particular age is the work of an artist. The tales of Frank are compositions of an artist with superlative craft; they are unusual and of obscure origin; they are impressive stories characterised by a familiar subject and a strange style. However they are not so much of the man as of the man-of-letters. Nevertheless, I am certain that Frank is capable of producing stories according to the eternal and primitive method; and I am equally sure that the result of his use of this method would be excellent stories and even more original ones—for, as I understand him, Frank is an original person. Some of his underlying themes are eternal, such as love and sorrow. Others have the trace of romantic sources, such as the social problems of the erotic personality; still others are psycho-analytical in nature, e.g., the erotic problem of the social personality.

2. In the conception of Frank, the science of esthetics comprises the entire science of man, and the most profound knowledge of man is that of art; therefore, man's life must be illuminated by esthetics; the mysteries of man must be revealed by art; and the destinies of man must be indicated by the artist. He professes a religious sense of art and an artistic sense of life; a mystic sense of nature and a naturalistic sense of religion. He believes in symbols, and being a naturalist he believes that symbols are born, that they live and that they die. If this be so, the extinct symbols must be replaced. As he is a mystic, he believes that the methods of art are symbolic; they are born, they live and they die. Therefore they must be replaced. He wishes to alter the rites of art—for he believes in the art of rites. But in this instance the temperament of the artist is the factor that determines the quality of the symbol; and the periodic mutation is here determined by the arguments of the essayist. However, art is not a religion, and does not make symbols. It is an expression and has only signs. And man in reality has only a religious sense of man, only a human

14

sense of life, and a vital sense of art: so that man confirms religion with his destiny, and with his life consecrates art. This religious sense, when professed toward all things, culminates in a religion of all things and the result is, according to the degree of culture attained, fetichism or pantheism. Actually, Frank is well versed in the precepts of Spinoza. A pantheistic ethics is the basis of his metaphysics. And because he considers (as the true artist would) that this doctrine is monistic, he makes of the mysterious relation of beings and things a natural religion of the union of beings and things; and a natural rite of the union of beings and things. He thus conceives an art from the unanimity of beings and things. But this copulation is enigmatic and this unanimity is hypothetical. Such a religion is emotional, the rite is instinctive, and the art is a mere hypostasis. Thus all that is religious in Frank is not religion but religiousness; all that is a symbol of mystery is not allegorical but spermatic; all that is a sign of art is not revelation but refraction. His conception is pantheistic, and his expression is usually uterine; his emotion is cosmic, and his realisation is generally phallic: he feels acutely the separation of beings, therefore he joins the sexes dionysiacally. He thus fulfills the rite of unity, and he accompanies the unity with the dithyramb.

3. Frank is an investigator and seeker in his art and wishes to give expression to the essential. Pantheism offers him one substance but this substance is conceived rather than perceived; it is meditated rather than expressed; it is inferred rather than made the object of experimentation. It is not dynamic but pacific; and what does not move and is not seen lacks plastic value. This is the problem of the pantheistic artist. He wishes to formulate an art of essence and at the same time express the essence of his art. But essences do not possess the power of motion; and the art of the novel is one of motion. As a matter of fact, in the novel and short story of Frank, all is movement; the impression is cinematographic, and the expression is rhythmic. Frank's art is one of snap-shots; it is expressionistic and does not make an impression of motives of permanence, but rather of motives of crises. He pursues substantial forms, but substance is formless, and he succeeds only in revealing spectral outlines. But in this, he is a discoverer. It thus occurs that a man who is a pantheist does not succeed in creating stories of pantheistic expression, precisely because he goes to the very heart of substance. He supplements this with lyricism which naturally is not convincing, because in the novel the novel must convince, not the poem. Pantheism may be a

doctrine, but it cannot produce an art: this is an additional proof that it is a false religion.[1] Pantheism claims that there exists one sole substance, but it offers not even one form; its phenomena are ideas rather than phenomena; its properties are ideas rather than properties; even its sensations are ideas rather than sensations. Pantheism is an emotion that interprets everything to accord with its own idea. But it is not a revelation, therefore it can translate nothing into forms. For that reason, when Frank dominates his subject he is not pantheistic, nor does he produce lyricism. He sees form, and he does not think of the substance; he is a realist and creates super-realism; then his intuition begins to function and he creates those active forms which a declamation in the spirit of Pan never could inspire. But he is also a naturalist; then a romantic refraction sets in and produces those ecstatical deformations which never result from a real vision.

But his naturalistic failing is not simple; it is mystic. Simple naturalism interprets man

[1] A false religion can produce an art, and then this art expresses a truth that the false religion is incapable of revealing; e.g., the ancient tragedy expresses a truth that the Greek religion could not reveal, and the novels and tales of Tolstoi express a Catholic truth that his laical religion was incapable of revealing and his discourse incapable of expounding. But when a religion cannot droduce an art, that fact alone proves it false, making further argument unneedful.

from the standpoint of the ape—according to
which there is nothing beyond the ape; thus
man's own nature is denied. Mystic naturalism considers man from the standpoint of the
angel. A spiritualistic and conscious pre-
sumption, justified by nothing, is attributed to
the angel; and the fact that man is a descendant
of Adam is ignored. Simple naturalism is
positivistic, and therefore does not distinguish
between man and ape. Mystic naturalism is
pantheistic and therefore makes no distinction
between the human spirit and the pure or
angelic spirit. Thus, simple naturalism admits
only the naturalistic in man and interprets
naturalistically all that tends toward the
spiritual. Mystic naturalism sees in man
only natural enjoyment and everything natural
is considered sublime. Simple naturalism is
bestial; mystic naturalism is diabolical: it is
characterised by pride in worldliness; it is
Spinoza and Rousseau; it is Hegelianism; it
is the strategem of the existent and the non-
existent; it is the conciliation of opposites; it is
the Dionysian euphoria, together with a metaphysical satyriasis. But the relations between
art and the devil are old; and so far as Waldo
Frank is concerned, Pan has not died.

4. The complex method used by Frank in his
tales and novels is theoretically unanimist, but
actually cinematographic. I must warn my

readers that I refer to the protagonists only in a conjectural way, since I am familiar only with their spectra; just as the naturalist speaks of matter only in a conjectural way because mathematically he is aware only of atoms and electrons. The initial presentation of the characters, as well as the introduction of physical motion, is a part of the plastic quality of the motion-picture. All consists of a movement of planes, each with its corresponding scene. With a sudden headlong rush the planes merge into one; sometimes they form a body, but the usual result is fusion rather than organization. And the scenes do not disclose episodes, but visions; the planes are dynamic, the visions are static and ecstatic. When the plane is projected well forward and is then brought to a halt, the scene becomes dynamic; the vision becomes an organized episode; action takes place and the moment is crucial. When a crisis occurs, Frank's short story and novel become revulsive; the characters suddenly become enormous and the tridimensional appearance which they assume distorts them. But like a snapshot the vision is perceived for just a moment. It is withdrawn immediately and another replaces it. The visions do not necessarily bear relation with one another, nor must any existing relationship be motivated. What transpires in several parts of one might occur in the same parts of any other, or in one section of many, according to the will of Frank. The characters in these stories lack fatality. But fatality is a requisite of art, for art is the work of man—not of God; and for this same reason in the Greek world where the gods were like men, fatality was dominant. In Frank's work, the personages do not possess freedom of moral will; yet they are absurdly free as regards their natural reaction. They lack conscience, and that alone is not bad— since Frank would have it so; but for that very reason they lack character, even though this is certainly not Frank's intention. They are psychoanalytic, but psychoanalysis does not always give them a psychology; because when they are lacking in a consciousness, they lack also an infra-consciousness. And when they do possess a consciousness, it is merely a speculative tendency—one that projects them toward fusion with the cosmos. They are not individual consciousnesses, avid of existence, but pantheistic ones, avid of substance. They represent cases rather than types; therefore psychoanalysis tints them, as it would specters, but does not define them as it would creatures. They constitute a series of schematisations of identical or different names; but the series is of greater import than the integers within it; the relative vision on the planes is of greater import than the series; and the movement of the series of planes is of greater significance than the plane. This movement of planes, these spectra of men, and this psychoanalytical projection of consciousness (as though achieved by means of reflectors) upon the planes in motion, with the visions following upon each other in rapid succession—this, in my estimation, is the art which Frank wishes to create.

I presume that Frank's conception of his characters is integral, although he represents them as disintegrated; as does the naturalist when he demonstrates that matter disintegrates into electrons. Frank does not make us witnesses of this disintegration; for he achieves it by means of his vision and only expresses the result of his vision. Thus, man merely appears discomposed, in a series of visions. These visions are illuminated in a series of planes; and the thoughts of man are like inscriptions on the plane; they are exhibited, they palpitate, they perform, on the same plane, and with as much ostentation as the man from whom, we gather, they have sprung, although we have not seen them make their appearance; for there is no process by means of which thought may be abstracted; but thought appears already disintegrated from the creature. However, these thoughts have rhythm, and the characters themselves do not always possess this quality. Thus, these thoughts of like rhythm maintain a greater unity than the visions of varied tempo. The planes, with their spectral figures, and with their voluminous thoughts are suddenly kindled—like a great flame which advances toward the spectator. It is like the vision which bears down upon one, on the moving picture series; and just at this moment, when the situation reaches its crisis, the last notion of a perspective is lost; everything becomes confused. The effect is identical with that made upon us by the advancing vision on the screen, which proceeded to the point where it almost touched us and then disappeared just as we were on the verge of believing that we felt it. Such is my impression of Frank's process. It is quite possible that with this process, profundity becomes an intimate experience; but it does not succeed in constituting a perspective.

5. The attempt has been made to compare Waldo Frank with James Joyce. But Joyce in respect to style is less modern, although he is a more matured artist. In Joyce, the characters have three dimensions; in Frank they assume the dimensions of the plane. In Joyce everything occurs within the character—for it has a body and a consciousness. In Frank everything occurs from without because the character is only a vision. In

Joyce, sensations and thoughts are all pre-
cipitated in the character; they occupy the
first plane, simultaneously; they emerge from
the past, they annul the relations of time and
make themselves felt.   All is seen from within
and all is present from within the character.
So even the remembrances, as memory has
created them, are present in their entirety
just as mental forms and physical stimuli are
present.   In Frank, sensations and thoughts
proceed in rhythmic, independent, free sen-
tences, separated from the characters.   Consciousness is projected outward upon a first
plane where it is seen alongside of the character, which may or may not be its owner,
since there is nothing to assure us of this
existing dependence (unless it be proximity on
the plane) or of communication between them.
The relation of time is annulled by advancing
the past toward the plane of the present; then
the vision is made immediate for the reader;
but this has nothing to do with the consciousness of the character.

In Joyce, all is present; in Frank, all is
instant.   In the former, the larvae of subconsciousness cause the play and internal
motive of the imagination.   In the latter, the
larvae of subconsciousness glow from afar upon
the planes in motion; like prepared larvae
made of metal.   Joyce is subjective but his

creatures are objective. Frank is objective
but the characters which he creates are to
human beings what the spectrum is to light.
The personages of Joyce, even when they have
no lustre, have volume. Frank's are like
illuminated specters.

But I do not consider this an esthetic
failure on the part of Waldo Frank; for it is a
result which he has achieved through his own
life experiences. Similar events are occurring
in other fields—physics for instance. The
more physics suffered from subjectivism, the
more volume it gave to matter; the more
objective it becomes and the more mathemati-
cal, the more it becomes diverted from matter.
Only the electron remains, and whether this is
matter or not is a problem still unsolved.
There are some who even suspect that matter
is a mere logical construction. Perhaps Frank
is on the point of revealing the same as true of
man. For Frank with his method of procedure
in the story and the novel is headed in this
direction: here, psychoanalysis is like a tincture
whose purpose is to illuminate and give substance to the lines of the spectrum.

Therefore, the problem of Joyce is one of
style and humor: *Ulysses* is to the naturalistic novel what *Don Quixote* was to the
novel of chivalry. But Frank's problem is
one of vision and life interpretation. This

super-realism of his is to realism what a radio-gram is to the organism.   But the radiograph is directed upon people whom one knows and to whom one bears some relation; and in these tales and novels one does not achieve relationship and unity with the people.   With such integration these experiences of art would be more than experiences of an artist; they would be art and new, as for example the new physics is new.   Then, the problem of time as it is represented in these experiences would also be important.   For Frank makes of time a subjective problem by which he proposes to objectify the heterogeneous qualities of time. Its nature may be expressed by these lines of Cardinal Newman:

"For spirits and men by different standards mete
   The less and greater flow of time.
   But intervals in their succession
   Are measured by the living thought alone
   And grow or wane with its intensity.
   And time is not a common property.
   But what is long is short and swift is slow,
   And near is distant, as received and grasped
   By this mind and by that."   *Dream of Gerontius*

Thus, Frank tends to achieve in the world of the novel and short story what Bergson achieves with time in the metaphysical realm and Einstein in the world of physics.   Frank is a relativist and his undertaking is good, because in my judgment the story and novel are, in their own way, *forms of knowledge*, no less than physics and metaphysics.

If one came to write as Joyce writes, one would be merely imitating Joyce. But if one came to regard things as Frank sees them, the short story and the novel would be transfigured. A new focus and new system of esthetic reference would be created; and the dimensions of volume would be reduced to the dimensions of the plane; the sensations of the body would be reduced to the vision of spectra, and the impressions of consciousness to the figures of a luminous placard. And that would be legitimate, if men were conceived spectrally, just as physics conceives light spectrally and matter electronically. But then, such a conception would have to be intuitive and not disintegrative.

6. Experiences of such great magnitude as these can be accredited only to a great writer, and in my estimation Frank is undoubtedly a great writer. There is genius in his style. His prose is rhythmic; his rhythms are varied, distinct, alternating, and profound; it is a prose which has gone to school to the Psalmist and to Walt Whitman. But it is prose, not verse. It is organic; its articulations are many, firm, and flexible; it is logical and it is metaphoric; its metaphor is a series of spontaneous

births of light, and its concepts resemble instruments of fine metal: they are delicate and hard, and they enrich the illumination. It is a style characterised by action. The passive elements of prose have been avoided. Its alliterations render it musical; they are sensitized but agreeable. It is a prose, harmonious yet not melodic; potent yet not eloquent. It is brilliant, but as a young body is brilliant, not an exquisite garment. It is firm and agile, like a young body. It is sensuous but gymnastic—impetuous yet serene. In my opinion, it is the best prose being written in the United States today.

Criterio, Buenos Aires

20

IDEAS ON WALDO FRANK

BY

ENRIQUE SERPA

Waldo Frank is—before all else—a man in function of totality.

Wholeness of thought, wholeness of emotion, wholeness of will, wholeness of love: all forms of wholeness are propitious to him and provide him with the means and substance of self-realization. With a rare gift for capturing the totality in things, in each event, he offers us the wholeness of his own mind and heart. In "living consciously within a Whole that holds all life," he touches the triple consummation to which a man may aspire: that of the poet, that of the philosopher, and that of the man himself.

Through his style—a style that is fervid, almost always direct, and gravid with sensuality and drama—there is revealed a man of conflicting passional motives. But the commanding passion is lucid and aseptic, the intricate currents are macerated by a serene philosophy: he is like a Dionysius converted to the esthetic of Apollo. His interior life is rich, complex, multiform, and saturated with subtle affects. Inevitably at times, it would burst forth in exaltation, that is to say, in a break-up of mental harmony, were it not for the repression of a clear intelligence and of a rapid and sure and subtle critical alertness. Often, his thought leaps into daring hazards and seems about to fall into Utopia. Thus when, in the rôle of ancient augur or of prophet, he foretells the coming of the new American, or when, with extraordinary psychological keenness, he reveals the seed of decadence in action, or when with protean wisdom he calmly pictures the political action, the literature, the arts and the mechanical progress of the United States as mere illusions. But always, he holds to a factual point for his departures, so that he manages to take his reader with him. He is like a gymnast, like the man of the circus who knows how to catch hold of the rope at the right moment, so as to run no risk of falling in his intricate acrobatics.

The new man of the Columbian continent must have the conviction, even if subconsciously, that he has seen the light in the land of the skyscraper and beneath the sign of technology. How deeply we need such modern men in our America, for our America—the America which, since Waldo Frank, and for such men as he, extends from Tierro del Fuego to the Arctic! These men, having learned technology, will go beyond it; respectful and understanding of matter, there will be body to their veneration of the spirit. From the harmonious convergence of these modes a psychic action will arise that will be true Americanism. For, as Waldo Frank has stated, the modern man, above all the man of America, cannot be hostile to the machine. But man's thought—above the machine and standardization—must be kept intact; for, as Pascal wrote, if man is but a reed, the weakest in Nature, yet he is a reed which thinks, which knows that it must die, and therefore, since it thinks and knows its destiny, superior to Nature.

An artist in the mystic sense, Frank reveres art religiously, as an organic living body. Like Dostoievski, Romain Rolland, José Martí, Miguel de Unamuno, Diego de Rivera, he confers upon it a transcendant rôle in the drama of the human spirit. Opposed to him is Ortega y Gasset proclaiming "art's dehumanization" and insisting that it be judged as a disinterested sport. Frank represents the authentic artist who suffers, in the flesh and in the spirit, the travail of creation; Ortega is the pure intellectual—flower of a decadent culture, more quickened to the aloof and external form of books than to the chaotic flow of life itself.

The contrast between these two men is

15

surprising. Ortega is Spanish and Frank is an American of the United States. One lives in the midst of a humanistic culture, saturate with art and passion, a culture which has given us Calderón, Saint Theresa, Goya, in the past and Unamuno, Baroja, Pérez Galdós, in the present. And the other lives in a tradition-less land, imperialistic, ironbound, where technology replaces art and the machine crowds out the man, the land where—to the outsider at least—the maximum human type appears to be a Ford, manufacturer of cheap motors.

In Spain, a Ganivet writes: "Often, meditating on the passion with which Spain has ever defended the doctrine of the Immaculate Conception, it has seemed to me that within this dogma there must be some mystery that is one with the mystery of our national soul: that perhaps this dogma is the admirable symbol of Spain's own life that, after the long and painful travail of maternity, comes in old age to find herself still virgin." And then, reveals his deep Hispanity in these words of Seneca: "Let not thyself be overcome by aught alien to thy spirit." . . . But on the other hand in the United States, Charles Lindbergh goes to such lengths in wooing the machine—the most strictly external of things, the most distant from the spirit, that he declares: "My airplane and I . . . *We*. . . ." And Henry

Ford in his book *My Life and Work* makes the following reflections: "We are getting to have a more precise understanding of reality, coming to know that in the world are all the preliminary means whereby we can win greater pleasure and abundance from life, and that we shall take advantage of the possibilities that offer to the extent that we interpret this reality properly and appreciate its importance." Can a more technical life evaluation be conceived? a more utilitarian ethics? Here in utter candor is proclaimed the narrowest mechanistic concept of the world. For Ford, life has no inherent, independent, subjective values. Quite the contrary: it is a sort of materialistic mine, out of which you must dig what you can. And from this vision rises the opponent of the traditional European norm: the Chauffeur materialistic, external, master and creature of the machine, whom Keyserling has described as the American type.

But now, against Lindbergh and his airplane, Ford and his flivver, rises Waldo Frank —with no attributes except a love formed of severity, grace, and understanding—the diamond-like clarity of a human soul. Those other men fulfill a function of power, and must subject themselves to the machine which is the symbol of their lust and which, using them, at the end cheats them of human plentitude and even of the comfort they demanded. Frank, through his function of culture and of love, masters both dream and action—the immediately material and the sublime—and harmonises them into a whole. He aspires to a precise and recondite knowledge of self, as the sole technology of freedom, since only from this knowledge will come to every man the awareness of what life is and of his function: together with the ability to act according to his knowledge.

Such, essentially, is Frank's message to the United States and to the American continents. And to this message, Hispanic-America responds with a fraternal sentiment toward the North—a sentiment which it has never felt before.

Excelsior, Habana

D. THE MAN

21

Waldo Frank on the Avenida

Yesterday, Waldo Frank had a rendezvous with the masses of Buenos Aires. The New York novelist, whose clever manipulation of shadows acquired human depth along the wharves of Riverside Drive, and in the oppressive sections of Manhattan, had wished to give his spirit, during one of our characteristic days, a profound and silent contact with our city. Thus he went forth, alone, into those streets filled with the ever-increasing excitation of restless faces. He wished both to observe and to feel. As he loves the Creole streets of our South, whose due praise he has won by describing for us the charm of New Orleans, he headed for the old borough of our city. Then he wished to see the crowds in all their festive mood in the Avenida de Mayo. And finally, finding it necessary to cross to an opposite sidewalk, he came up against the guard whose impersonal zeal was shown in the wire he was holding, against any and all. A rebellious spirit always finds a way out, and taking advantage of the carelessness of the policeman whose human nature makes itself evident at times, either by his admiration for the parade or even by his immersion in thought,—the North American author slipped from the sidewalk, ready to put into effect the difficult crossing.

Then three policemen, fox hounds of the law, pursued him, and Waldo Frank found himself violently questioned, surrounded and stared at. But it was his intention to have the taste of a bitter experience as a necessary prelude to a better love, and Mr. Frank passively allowed himself to be reprimanded.

A high police official, all gallooned, approached the group that had gathered about the gesticulating gloves of public order, and entered into the argument. And while the group of spectators was increasing, a timid voice was suddenly heard. An elderly spectator said: "It's Waldo Frank." The public repeated, "It's Waldo Frank," and as the author smiled calmly, all the policemen fearfully protested in chorus to their officer.

"And if he is Waldo Frank, why doesn't he say so?"

Smiling, Waldo Frank assented; and then and there, in the densely crowded Avenida de Mayo an ovation burst forth.

The representatives of authority must then have felt a literary thrill—a vague suggestion

of the confluence of the mysteries of art; and
the author of *City Block* crossed the street
accompanied by the profound obeisance of
three representatives of the public order.
Everybody, on seeing him, understood that
now it was a case of three policemen in the
custody of an author.

La Nación, Buenos Aires

22

WALDO FRANK OR THE GIFT OF SYMPATHY

On very few occasions, other than the series
of lectures that the North American writer,
Waldo Frank, has been giving among us, has
the gift, rare among intellectuals of his high
quality, of holding the attention of his audience
been so clearly manifest.

The enjoyment of listening and the eagerness
to understand him whereby our public pays
its absolute homage are really most unusual.
Neither the lecturer's extensive culture nor the
interest in his themes would be sufficient to
evoke it.   No.   From the very first moment,
there rises from the literary composition and
flows towards the public a stream of sympathy
so deep, so cordial, that it alone can explain
this rare phenomenon; the ardent desire on the
part of his audience to listen and imperturbably
to understand.

The   above-mentioned   author—an   artist
above all, lest we forget it—possesses in fact,
and to a degree approaching the religious
plane, the gift of emotional sympathy through
which a spiritual comprehension can be so

easily reached. His thought may differ from ours, one may or may not agree with what he says; but we are always certain that he doesn't try to distract his audience with fine paradoxes. Thus does this man, and herein lies the secret of his ability to arouse our interest—give the clear impression that he himself believes what he is saying.

Every quality of the lecturer revolves around this center of sincerity. He is the first to be convinced by the warm quality of his opinion: if he errs, the man, his spirit and his heart together err. The presence among us of this American, representative of an idealistic and somewhat transcendental race is deeply gratifying to us.

La Nación, Buenos Aires

23

My Friendship with Waldo Frank

Alfonso Reyes
Mexican Ambassador to Argentina

My friendship with Waldo Frank has four acts, and each one in a different city.

The first act took place in Madrid, in the spring of 1924. Frank was gathering the impressions and documents for his *Virgin Spain*. I gave him a letter to the Mexican painter, Angel Zárraga, who lives in Paris; it seemed natural to me that these two men should meet, who had a certain affinity in the pure intention of their lives, in their youthfulness, in their scarcely definable way, of being brave without loss of sweetness, and in the brotherhood of their gaze and open hand. From that first meeting with Waldo Frank resulted a message to the writers of Mexico (the first contact of Waldo Frank with our America), which I had the pleasure of delivering, myself.

The second act took place in New York a few months later. I was on my way to Europe on an urgent mission. Frank conducted me to a little terrace, in the publishing house of Boni and Liveright, which formed an oasis of literary conversation, submerged in the midst of a mountainous desert of walls, high, black, and melancholy.

The third act was set later in Paris, in the room of a hotel. Both of us felt that our friendship had ripened rapidly, and I believe that we forged some plans that were to lead to better mutual understanding between the two Americas.

The first time I was on the point of leaving Spain; the second, I was about to leave for Europe; the third, I was just returning from Paris. We had always, up to now, conversed, as it were, in the midst of suitcases; in those instants of a journey, when conversation seems almost to be a testament, a last wish. Therefore, perhaps, we hastened to tell one another all. Each meeting had been like a new pact. Furthermore, we were brought closer to each other by the old ideals of human cordiality, and by our faith in the distinct destiny of America. We were moreover bound to each other by the mysterious numbers of Time; a superstition which I have so often considered important, for we both saw the light in 1889. I leave this matter to the astrologers.

Once when discussions on the crisis between our respective national interests had become dangerous and bitter, I telegraphed to Waldo Frank from Paris to Berlin: "Speak, my friend, in the name of our common ideals." Waldo

Frank was absent and received my message very late. Then he sent me an answer by letter which I shall always lovingly treasure. "As yet I have no authority," he told me, "to intervene in these affairs which I have not mastered. But have confidence in me. If I have come close to Spain, it was because I wished to enter by that royal road of history into Hispano-America."

And he has fulfilled this promise. He learned Spanish. He was in Mexico. Now he goes to Argentina.

The desire to be a few hours more with Colonel Sidar brought me to Montevideo. My aviator left this morning, headed for Brazil. On consulting the boats for my return to Buenos Aires, I discovered that the Voltaire arrived and was sailing today, too. I remembered that Waldo Frank was on board. And at this hour the two of us together are contemplating the waters of the Rio de la Plata, going over reminiscences and auguries, and taking the cabalistic computation of all the incidences and providential signs that have accompanied our friendship, which we should like to see as the symbol of the friendship between the two Americas.

On board the S. S. *Voltaire*,
    Montevideo, Sept. 22, 1929

El Espectador, Bogotá

24

THE SUCCESS OF WALDO FRANK IN BUENOS AIRES

Unanimity of the Homage of the Intellectuals of Argentina

Even those in Buenos Aires who knew best the work of Waldo Frank, the remarkable originality of his thought, could not foretell the unique success of his lectures in the leading universities of Argentina. Neither Ortega y Gasset nor Keyserling—both preceded by an older renown—had a triumph as complete as Waldo Frank in Buenos Aires. The great North American has merited the applause of the universitarian and academic sectors—(he visited Buenos Aires specially invited by the University) and of the artistic and literary, journalistic and Bohemian sectors. The daily press of Buenos Aires has followed his magnificent lectures with an interest that reflected not alone the attention due the author of *The Rediscovery of America*, but as well the resonance of his personal popularity in Buenos Aires.

This success is explained not only by the union in Waldo Frank of a penetratingly modern thinker with an exquisite artist, but rather by the wave of sympathy which the man aroused by virtue of the congruence of his thoughts with the most subtle intuitions of his public. Waldo Frank is a man full of youth and humanity, whose vital North American traits are enhanced by a culture and intelligence, as far removed as possible from the mediocrity of the standardized and pragmatic Yankee.

After giving eight masterly lectures in the University—lectures that gained him the most extensive admiration in Buenos Aires as a master of the fundamental themes of America, Waldo Frank has proceeded to Rosario, which waits to hear him. He will visit the principal cities of the Argentine Republic, a country that has interested him perhaps because Frank notices in the formation of Argentina elements very similar to those in the formation of the United States.

The Argentine government placed at the disposal of Frank a special train for his trip through the country, but Frank declined this offer. He said that he was not an aristocrat and that he preferred, in accord with a more modern practice, to travel as a swallow.

The homages to which Waldo Frank has been an object on the part of the Argentine intellectuals have been characterized by a tone of absolute spontaneity. *La Vida Literaria* dedicated a number to him, which will be followed by one of *Sintesis*. And everyone has agreed that the things and men of North America have never been appraised with keener understanding than on the occasion of the lectures of Frank.

El Mundo, Lima

25

Waldo Frank in Lima

Thanks to our friend, José Carlos Mariátegui, we have received some echoes of the extraordinary reception which the intelligentsia of Lima extended in tribute to Waldo Frank, as well as an authentic copy of the text of Presentation which the Committee of Welcoming Writers and Artists has had printed in the Program of his Lectures.

It is with pleasure that we transcribe this presentation and promise our readers to publish in our next number a notice on the visit of Waldo Frank to Havana.

Presentation

"Shunning a protocol, the Committee of Welcoming Writers and Artists will forego the discourse of presentation in his lectures. The attention of the public on occasions like this is directed wholly toward the lecturer. In anxious tension, the public wishes to hear only his words. Every intermediary only serves to emphasize this, no matter how discreetly he may play his part. The address of presentation does not serve, in general, as a sentimental preparation for the audience. Its object more

226

or less is the superfluous laudation or polishing off of the orator. The sentimental preparation of the audience is not obtained by a flash of rhetorical hodge-podge.

Waldo Frank is visiting us without standing on ceremony. He has come to Lima at the request of the intellectuals and artists who have admired him since the first reading of his works. We have a sense of almost being obliged to see to it that this atmosphere of friendliness which no protocol embarrasses is preserved to the end of his visit. If this is an innovation, Waldo Frank deserves it.

"The bio-bibliographical record of Waldo Frank, reduced to its simplest terms, is as follows: He was born in New Jersey in 1889. He is about forty years old. His youth was formed in part in Europe, or under the influence of things European. But Waldo Frank kept himself, in spite of his European experience, essentially American. By the time he was fifteen the work of Walt Whitman had become his bible both poetic and political. Europe did not master him but he had assimilated Europe profoundly. And from Europe, he departed for the conquest, for the possession of America. No one has put such determination and such intelligence into this undertaking. He began his career as a novelist with *The Unwelcome Man* (1917). His second book revealed the esthete and the essayist, *The Art of the Vieux Colombier* (1918).

"But the renown through both America and Europe which he has earned, he owes to *Our America* (1919) with its extraordinary interpretation of the United States. A genial certitude of his thirty years preceded his celebrity at forty. In the prologue written for the Spanish-American edition of this book Frank says that 'it was the first to conquer the attention of the intellectual world' and 'in a sense altogether more profound' he adds, 'the first, because it contains the essence and spirit of my literary message.' *The Rediscovery of America* (1929), the latest of the books of Waldo Frank, continues during the next ten years the task begun with *Our America*, and, among other books, *Virgin Spain* (1924) is the first station of the journey which today brings Waldo Frank to Peru.

This free American, as Sanin Cano, one of the thinkers of Latin America who most esteem him, would say of him, feels profoundly the unity of America. The rediscoverer of America could not stop with the explanation of the United States. And he approaches Spain 'so as to enter by the royal road of history into Hispano-America.'

"These three books of Waldo Frank are the only ones today translated into our language. But the work of Waldo Frank, without counting the two books above-mentioned, is much more. Frank excels in fiction, in the novel. He is the author of *The Dark Mother* (1920), *Rahab* (1923), *Chalk Face* (1924). Through his stories and novels, there flows the same pure blood of the artist which runs through his works of history and philosophy. He is a profound exponent of the life of North America. He attains the complete possession of its innermost and most fertile secrets. Frank's novels have, like his essays, a poetic accent. Frank, in the novel, tends to realize always the poem. The list of his works is completed with *Salvos* (1924), *Time Exposures* (1926), and *New Year's Eve* (1929).

"In Frank there is contained and concentrated the most perfect combination of the gifts of the thinker and the artist. His thought has a symphonic expression. His force and his creative art work on a culture richly embellished and modern. The construction of America, because America is yet to be created, is in great part, for him, an esthetic enterprise. And all of this he feels and expresses with the sentiment and discipline of the artist.

"He is a representative of the North American spirit, because he prolongs it. He does not take refuge in its tradition; he proceeds from it and clarifies and continues it. His attitude is always that of a hopeful creator.

If Goethe proposed to Europe the ideal of the 'good European,' Waldo Frank proposes to us with original eloquence and in appropriate language the ideal of the 'good American.'

"To learn to understand us, he has come to us by the 'royal road' of Spain. He has started on his journey. Not only is he one of the most admirable thinkers of modern times, but he is more particularly one of ours. He is one of the fighters, one of the mentors of an America of which we have many trivial versions, and of which he is going to offer us in these lectures a profound interpretation. Let us listen to his message!"

La Vida Literaria, Buenos Aires

26

How Waldo Frank Speaks

"This is the third time that I have learned Spanish," Waldo Frank tells us. "The first time was when I was in Spain, and I thought I had learned it. Afterward I went to Mexico, and great was my disillusion. My Castilian wouldn't do. And now I see that here I must learn Argentine." For these and for other reasons it is very interesting to say something about how Waldo Frank speaks. In reading his lectures he has a little of the sing-song accent of the pupil who has learned his lesson well. At times he makes a mistake in pronunciation and repeats the paragraph again; a word of more than three syllables, when it is accented on the antepenult, is a very difficult obstacle for him to conquer. The recurring preoccupation of the writer is to pronounce Castilian well; and that, queer as it may seem, is when he is least clearly understood. But when he allows himself to be moved by passion, by the spiritual contents, by the enthusiasm of what he is expressing, then he forgets this preoccupation, and the word reaches the hearer more vibrant and clear.

The North American writer's eagerness to

speak Spanish is praiseworthy. It introduces
into his speech a significant homage of friendship which should not go unrecognized, because it is, without a doubt, one more task
which the man of letters imposes on himself,
and which doubtless will greatly complicate
his labors. It is a mode which Keyserling
imposed, but which Frank follows with all
severity.

Hitherto, foreign lecturers have not conde-
scended to speak Spanish, not for anything in
the world; it seemed to them something that
violated their personality. In this the most
disdainful were the French, who believed that
the whole universe was obliged to know French.
But an Anglo-Saxon and a German have set
the example, and henceforth we shall see
lecturers trying to make themselves understood in Spanish.

When he refers to the future of America,
Frank has a Messianic accent. He speaks
then as though gazing on a vision which appears
before him. His tone is prophetic and vibrant
with a contagious fervor. In this his race is
revealed. It seems that his voice comes from
the depths of the centuries to speak the
opportune word in the midst of present chaos.
For he, above all, is the man of the word.

And it is thus that one hears him speak.
Immobile, with no pantomime, all the efficacy

of what he says is in his precision and tonality.
In all things he is an artist who knows
dramatically that beauty is a purification of
all artifice. Thus you have him on the
platform, as if he were a Responder, to use the
term that would be pleasing to the author of
Leaves of Grass. He is one who comes with
the good news—who comes from the North
and goes toward the future.

How does Waldo Frank speak? ask the
people who have not heard him. And we
could answer them by saying: Frank is among
the first Americans who have existed; that is
to say, he is the American of both North and
South who will be the future man of this
continent. His voice is foreign and at the
same time friendly; surprising and at the same
time intimate. He speaks of things that will
be, of a future seen imperfectly through all
the chaotic pasts and the crumbled Utopias of
politicians without fortunes and millionaires
without intelligence. The voice of Waldo
Frank is that of the prophetic brother who,
from the highest tower of his illusion, sees into
the future. Thus speaks Waldo Frank.

Critica, Buenos Aires

27

The Message and the Man

Onto the platform of the Faculty of the Humanities, of *La Plata*, comes a little man of modest demeanor and natural gestures. There is in him a certain mysterious resemblance to the ingenious and sad little man who is Charles Chaplin. He begins his talk: "Sisters and brothers." He speaks, sincerely, artlessly, with a passion tempered by a warm accent, and in a tone like that of a distant or muted instrument. He describes the ascending trajectory of American ideals in recent years. He tells of the rebellion of youth, its defeat and resignation. A quarter of a century of spiritual revolt has come to naught; but the failure cannot be conclusive. The background of his words is dark and tremorous; the picture itself is painted in cool, courageous, wrathful colors.

We are in the presence of an historical event—one of the kind which at times descends from the page of legend or fiction to become fact before our eyes. In the twenty-ninth year of this century of changes, a humble man, a man without deceit, an eminent artist in word and thought, comes to us from the most feared and powerful country upon earth, to confess to us, in candor and in grief, the spiritual failure of his country—giant North America. This event holds a new beauty, which history heretofore has never known.

Waldo Frank, the *Nucleo Diógenes*—a sheet modest and obscure, yet not unlit with spirit, answers your disconsolate words: the People which has a son so self-forgetting that he could accomplish this miracle of truth and heroism, is—whatever be its faults—a living hope for mankind.

Diógenes, La Plata

A WALDO FRANK

POR

EZEQUIEL MARTÍNEZ ESTRADA

(Oh, capitán, mi capitán!
Bien sé que ya otras veces nos vimos—hace tiempo,
aquí o allá—;
creo que en un combate o en una larga marcha,
o en un buque de guerra, en alta mar,
o en alguna cabaña, una noche oscurísima
de lluvia, de temporal,
en que era menester proteger—no recuerdo
ya bien qué nobles cosas—algo en la oscuridad.
Tú impartías las órdenes, tú mandabas la tropa,
oh, capitán, mi capitán!)

Poetas!: él es nuestro camarada que llega,
es un cantor de América—es un alma, y no más.
Aquel que esté dispuesto a dar lo que posee
—riqueza, juventud, amor, renombre, paz—
aquel que sea rápido, y ágil, y esté resuelto;
aquel que sea intrépido, viril y alto y audaz;
aquel que se halle sano y sea generoso;
aquel que tenga anhelos de ser mejor y más;
aquel que ame en América la tierra del futuro,
del cuerpo y del espíritu, material e ideal;
que abandone las aulas, si estudia; que abandone
su taller, si trabaja—deje amigos y hogar—
pues a todos nosotros, uno a uno (uno a uno
él nos conoce a todos) a todos nombrará,
y es preciso estar prontos y responder: "Presente,
mi capitán!"

236

No haremos una tropa de valetudinarios
—que los lisiados queden donde están:
el tísico en su hamaca, el luético en su cama,
el epiléptico en su sofá,
el cojo en sus muletas, el tullido en su silla,
el manco en su manquedad,
el ciego en su tiniebla, el huérfano en su asilo,
el ladrón en su celda, el anciano en su hogar,
el mudo en su penumbra, el ebrio en su cuneta,
el lascivo en su lupanar,
el idiota en su ergástula, en su banco el inválido,
el hospitalizado en su hospital,
(ya llegará el momento de ocuparnos de ellos,
después o nunca más;)
haremos una tropa sana, valiente, alegre,
un ejército joven, altruista y veraz,
amante de la vida y amante de la muerte,
del bien y del mal,
respetuoso de todo lo que ya tiene forma
pero infinitamente más
respetuoso de aquello que aún no ha logrado forma,
que está por ser, y que será,
de jóvenes que ansíen los puestos de vanguardia
(porque hay montañas que trepar,
millas que hacer a nado, páramos infinitos
de sed, fatiga y soledad,
selvas inextricables que a tajo de machete
hemos de desbrozar, de talar, de allanar,
pantanos, salitrales, punas alucinantes,
bosques llenos de fieras y todo lo demás)
porque hay cien mil peligros, más de cien mil peligros
que afrontar
con la sola esperanza de conquistar un día
lo mismo que tenemos, con más seguridad.
¿Quién sabe a dónde iremos, ni cuál es la consigna,
ni cuál la dirección en que partir, ni cuál
el río que vadeemos, la cumbre que alcancemos,

ni el erial (ni el erial
donde en el canjilón del cráneo la hemorragia
nos brinde el agua agónica de un febril hontanar)
que crucemos exhaustos? (No obstante, estoy
seguro, oh, capitán, mi capitán!)
¿Sabemos qué ciudades magníficas, qué chozas
hemos de defender o de asaltar?
¿sabemos qué metrópolis habrán de demolerse,
qué templos, qué edificios, qué estatua colosal,
qué cárceles, qué escuelas hemos de echar abajo
para pasar la reja del arado y sembrar,
o en qué paraje aislado alzaremos de nuevo
la ciudad y las cosas que forman la ciudad?

Acaso algunos queden, robustos y admirables,
con la herramienta antigua, en la heredad,
cultivando los árboles que los padres plantaron
o bien en el umbral
saludando a lo lejos a los soldados líricos
que se van.
(Acaso, hacia la tarde, en una luz violeta
oh, piadoso deber filial y fraternal—,
queden algunos jóvenes sepultando a sus muertos,
o reparando el muro que abatió el huracán,
o estudiando en los libros las lecciones de siempre,
o aprendiendo los versos que habrán de recitar;
ajustando en el eje la rueda remendada,
embadurnando el techo de alquitrán,
azuzando a sus perros contra la vaca ajena,
curándole la sarna al recental.)
Nosotros ya estaremos tramontando la loma,
unidos para siempre—tropa sana y cordial—,
homéricos, "en orden y respirando fuerza,"
oh, capitán, mi capitán!

Septiembre 19, 1929

La Vida Literaria, Buenos Aires

III. A BANQUET IN NEW YORK

On Waldo Frank's return to the United States, his friends and admirers felt that his triumph in Hispano-America was a fit occasion for honoring him with a dinner in testimony of his achievements as an artist and a writer and a leader. The dinner was given under the auspices of the "Institute of International Education," in the Ball Room of the Hotel Roosevelt, in New York City, on the evening of February 17, 1930. The Sponsors were Mrs. Samuel Sloan Auchincloss, the Marquesa de Belmont, Mr. Bruce Bliven, Prof. Franz Boas, Mr. Frank Bohn, Mr. Raymond L. Buell, Mr. Herbert Croly, Prof. Frank Callcott, Sr. José Camprubí, Prof. J. P. Chamberlain, Mr. Charles Chaplin, Prof. John Dewey, Dr. John Finley, President Glenn Frank, Mr. Hubert Herring, Mr. Jerome Hess, Mr. Charles D. Hurrey, Prof. Louis Imbert, Dr. Samuel Guy Inman, Mr. Otto H. Kahn, Mr. Willard V. King, Prof. Samuel McCune Lindsay, Mr. Lewis Mumford, Prof. Federico de Onís, Prof. E. Allison Peers, Mr. Maxwell Perkins, Mr. George A. Plimpton, Mrs. Arthur Sachs, Mr. Alfred Stieglitz, Mrs. Susan Huntington Vernon.

Dr. Stephen P. Duggan presided, as President of the "Institute of International Education" and as representative of the "Instituto de las Españas." Professor Onís spoke on "Waldo

*Frank as an Interpreter of Spanish Culture";
Mr. Lewis Mumford's address was entitled
"Waldo Frank as an Interpreter of the Civilization of the United States"; Mr. Otto Kahn spoke
on "Waldo Frank as an American Leader";
and Mr. Frank's subject was "What is Hispano-America to us?"*

*We have omitted the addresses of Mr. Mumford
and Mr. Kahn, since they dealt with the more
general aspects of Mr. Frank's work as an
American artist and thinker; whereas the subject
of this volume includes only his relations with
Hispano-America.*

Waldo Frank and Spanish Civilization

Federico de Onís

This occasion affords me the very gratifying
opportunity of expressing my thoughts about
Waldo Frank's Hispanic activities; but I hope
you will all understand that in this moment I
represent nobody. The only representative
value my words can have is that of voicing
the reactions of one of many Spaniards to the
labor of a man of original thought and superior
mentality, who belongs to another nation and
another civilization, and who for years, with
growing intensity, has been devoting his
serious, absorbed, comprehensive attention
to the civilization of which I am a product.

In all times Spain and the American countries that inherited her civilization have been
accustomed to awaken among significant figures
of other nations curiosity, interest and love for
the unique realities of our life and our history,
for the mode of being which we and our tradition represent. But it has been still more
frequent for them to encounter superficiality,
lack of understanding, and disdain born of and
nourished by age-old prejudices. The fact

243

that the admirers and interpreters of our
civilization in foreign lands are few, but, at
the same time, unusual and original personalities who think for themselves and are capable
of disentangling their thoughts from the web of
trite commonplaces, goes to show that the
Spanish reality is difficult of comprehension
because different, and because it is a unique
creation, in the face of which there are only
two possible positions: to understand it or not;
to grow spiritually richer through contact with
it, or to close one's eyes to it,—an attitude of
love or of hate. This is why it so frequently
happens that the foreigner who approaches
Spain for the first time has the sensation of
making a discovery; and why he feels rising,
out of the night of prejudice and negation
which made up his early ideas of Spain and
Spanish America, the vision of one of the
clearest, most harmonious and dynamic human
worlds that have ever existed.

If I am not mistaken, this has been Waldo
Frank's experience. From his early years he
has shown himself capable of creating his
own ideas, of not yielding to those the milieu
offered him. Following his years of formation
in this America, his restless, questing spirit,
full of intellectual and esthetic problems,
leads him to the civilization of Europe, and
directs him toward its two great beacon lights:

German thought and French art. France, "the heart of Europe," as he has called it, wins his affections; nowhere does he find such a perfect, complete and exquisite realization of Western civilization, that is to say, of his own. But if his contact with this middle-European world, the one most akin to the American and Anglo-Saxon civilization of which he is a product, enriched him, on the one hand, with its magnificent creations, which are the result of the accumulated density of centuries; on the other hand, it lowered him in his own self-esteem, as he contemplated the differences of quality between European civilization in its own home and the products of its expansion in America. He could not help measuring the realities of his own land with the yardstick of his critical consciousness, and the result produced a certain dissatisfaction in him.

Nothing could be more remote from me than to criticize this attitude in a person or in a nation. A conscious, active dissatisfaction which stimulates the individual or collective spirit is an unfailing symptom of superiority, just as a smug satisfaction with things as they are is evidence of sterile mediocrity which leads to nothing. The fruit of this attitude in Frank is *Our America*, which reflects his vision of his own country after his spiritual encounter with Europe and France.

17

Spain as yet does not exist for him. His first contact with her is casual. As one who, after living in a city, should visit its outskirts in order to know it more completely, so Frank begins his first visit to Spain, one of Europe's suburbs. Perhaps besides this desire to round out his acquaintance with Europe, there was also a vague curiosity about the mysterious, the unknown, for so subtle a spirit as his could not fail to perceive the inconsistencies and contradictions in his ideas about Spain. His first contact with Spain the unknown, his relations with its people, his reading of its books are a revelation to him, and amount to the discovery of a new world, different from all the rest of Europe. The essence of his experience fills the pages of *Virgin Spain,* which is the most moving book that any foreigner has ever written about Spain, and in which, as he exalts Spain, Frank reaches the heights of his own soul's exaltation.

It is beside the point to enter here upon a discussion of his interpretation; many of the details may be controversial—and one characteristic of everything Spanish is that it is a motive of endless controversy—but the vision in its totality is true and penetrating. Frank's poetic perception conveys to us as no other has done the true reality of Spain, the dramatic reality of a nation which ever consists not in what it is but in what it wills to be. The essence and the oneness of Spain lie in its will, its dynamic force, its striving for the effort's sake, its aspiration both unattainable and invincible. This explains the unchanging virginity of Spain, the country of Europe which has suffered the most external vicissitudes, all of which however have passed over her like the conceiving of the Mother of God or the light through glass, without breaking or soiling her. Each time the hidden force of her indomitable reality, her capacity for aspiring, her will, have emerged purer than ever.

And this American-European Frank, who has dreamed the dream of Spain, the dream of the Cid and of Isabel and of Don Quijote and of Segismundo and of Unamuno—and of the Castilian peasants whom, in never to be forgotten hours, we visited together, in the landscape of their evergreen oaks, where graze those noble bulls who teach them to meet death face to face—, will never awaken from it. He will return to his America and will feel himself more American than ever because Spain, the Faustic nation par excellence—to employ Spengler's terminology—has taught him that what counts is not results but possibilities, the impulses which create the realities of tomorrow; that life consists not in being but in aspiring, in the determination to be oneself.

And this impressive example of Frank's reveals
to us that like him all America, if it has received from Germany models of science and
organization, and from France finished and
exquisite models of art and life—models which
are admirable but often inimitable and exclusive—can receive from Spain the most
generous and useful gift of all: a consciousness
of its own worth and a faith and pride in itself,
the impulse to take its place in the world of
the future where we may all be equals. For
this reason, after *Virgin Spain* Frank writes
his *Rediscovery of America*, of the America
that aspires to be.

And from these two conceptions, the drama
of Spain and the vast and generous ideal of
America, comes his interest in Spanish America
and his recent trip to these countries, which is
the reason for our gathering here tonight.
Not long ago Spanish America was still more
unknown to him and seemed more incongruous
and contradictory than Spain had before; a few
months sufficed for Frank to accomplish in
Spanish America a labor of approximation
and understanding such as has never been seen
before, and which I am sure will bear fruit
endlessly both in Spanish America and in
Frank's own spirit. The countless, well-inten-
tioned North American attempts to achieve
an understanding between the two Americas

have been, if not entirely, almost fruitless. All North Americans interested in Spanish America—and all should be—must know that Waldo Frank's trip to Hispanic America has been more successful and will have more lasting results, than that of any of the outstanding intellectual figures of the whole world who have visited those countries. North Americans should not only be proud, but should study this fact like a lesson. There is food for thought in it for all of us. To me it seems evident that, aside from his exceptional individual qualities, Waldo Frank has reached the very heart of the Spanish Americans because he came to them, after having passed through Spain, with a sincere, profound and generous ideal of America, an ideal in whose profundities may be felt the pulsation of the Spanish spirit.

The end